Grammar Practice

Grade 10

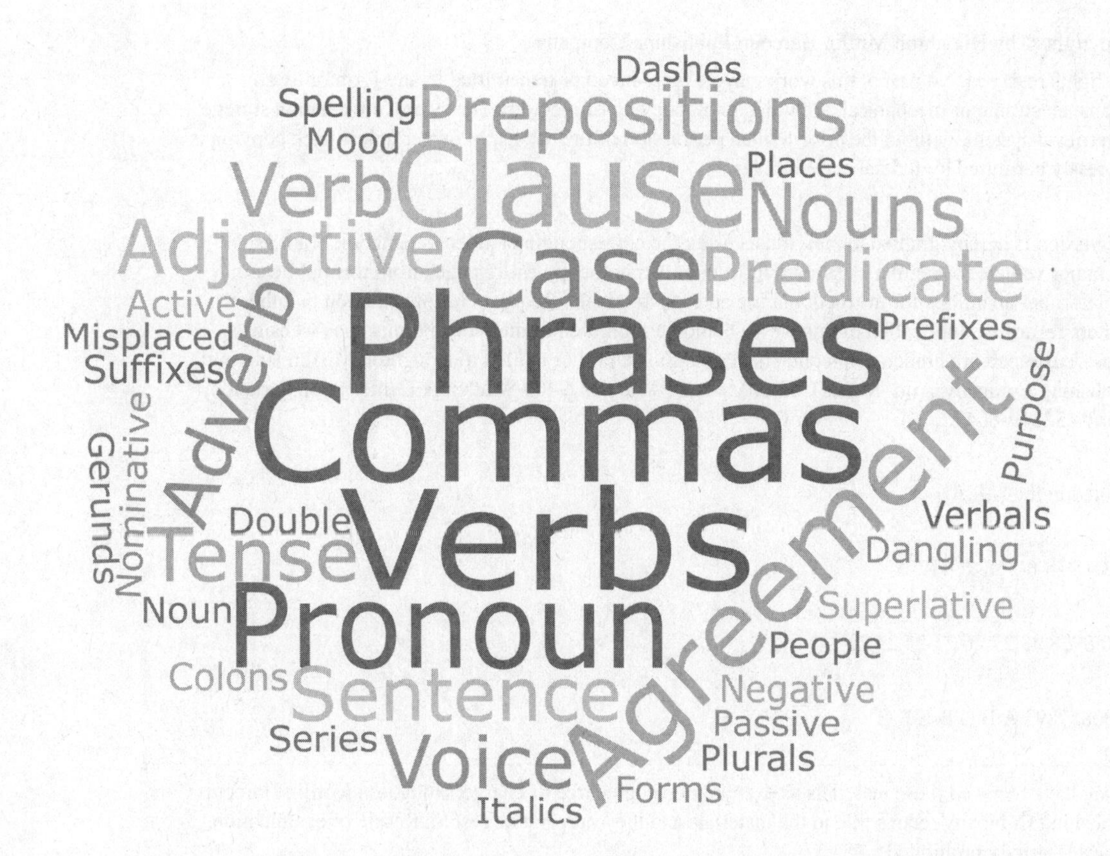

Printed in the U.S.A.

ISBN 978-0-358-26417-0

9 10 0928 28 27 26 25 24 23 22

4500857893 A B C D E F G

Table of Contents

Module 1 **PARTS OF SPEECH**

Nouns 1
Compound Nouns 3
Pronouns 5
Adjectives 7
Pronouns and Nouns Used as Adjectives 9
■ Review Exercise 11
Verbs 13
Linking Verbs 15
The Verb Phrase 17
Adverbs 19
Adverbs Modifying Adjectives and Other Adverbs 21
Prepositions 23
Conjunctions and Interjections 25
■ Module Review 27

Module 2 **THE SENTENCE**

Sentences and Sentence Fragments 29
Run-on Sentences 31
Subject and Predicate 33
The Simple Subject and Predicate 35
Finding the Subject 37
Compound Subjects and Compound Verbs 39
Complements 41
Subject Complements 43
Objects 45
Classifying Sentences by Purpose 47
■ Module Review 49

Module 3 **THE PHRASE**

Prepositional Phrases 51
Adjective Phrases and Adverb Phrases 53
Verbals and Verb Phrases 55
Participial Phrases 57
Gerunds 59
Gerund Phrases 61
Infinitives and Infinitive Phrases 63
■ Review Exercise 65
Appositives and Appositive Phrases 67
■ Module Review 69

Module 4	**THE CLAUSE**	
	Kinds of Clauses	**71**
	The Adjective Clause	**73**
	The Adverb Clause	**75**
	The Noun Clause	**77**
	Sentence Structure	**79**
	■ Module Review	**81**
Module 5	**AGREEMENT**	
	Number	**83**
	Subject-Verb Agreement	**85**
	Intervening Phrases	**87**
	Agreement with Indefinite Pronouns	**89**
	Compound Subjects	**91**
	Collective Nouns	**93**
	■ Review Exercise 1	**94**
	Other Problems with Agreement	**95**
	■ Review Exercise 2	**97**
	Pronoun Agreement	**99**
	■ Module Review	**101**
Module 6	**USING PRONOUNS CORRECTLY**	
	Case of Pronouns	**103**
	The Nominative Case	**105**
	The Objective Case	**107**
	Objects of Prepositions	**109**
	■ Review Exercise	**111**
	Who and *Whom*	**113**
	Other Pronoun Problems	**115**
	Inexact Pronoun Reference	**117**
	■ Module Review	**119**
Module 7	**USING VERBS CORRECTLY**	
	Regular Verbs	**121**
	Irregular Verbs	**123**
	Verb Tense	**127**
	Consistency of Tense	**131**
	Active Voice and Passive Voice	**133**
	Lie and *Lay*	**135**
	Sit and *Set* and *Rise* and *Raise*	**137**
	■ Module Review	**139**

Module 8 **USING MODIFIERS CORRECTLY**

Comparison of Modifiers **141**
Uses of Comparative and Superlative Forms **143**
Dangling Modifiers **145**
Misplaced Modifiers **147**
■ Module Review **149**

Module 9 **A GLOSSARY OF USAGE**

Accept, Except / At **151**
Being As, Being That / Invent, Discover **153**
Kind, Sort, Type / Should Of **155**
Some, Somewhat / Would Of **157**
The Double Negative **159**
■ Module Review **161**

Module 10 **CAPITAL LETTERS**

People and Places **163**
School Subjects, First Words, Proper Adjectives **165**
Groups, Organizations, and Religions **167**
Objects, Events, Awards **169**
Titles **171**
■ Module Review **173**

Module 11 **PUNCTUATION I**

End Marks **175**
Abbreviations **177**
■ Review Exercise **178**
Commas in a Series **179**
Punctuating Independent Clauses **181**
Commas with Nonessential Elements **183**
Commas with Introductory Elements **185**
Commas with Other Sentence Interrupters **187**
Other Uses of Commas **189**
■ Module Review **191**

Module 12 **PUNCTUATION II**

Semicolons **193**
Colons **195**
Underlining (*Italics*) **197**
Quotation Marks **199**
■ Review Exercise **202**
Apostrophes **203**
Dashes and Parentheses **205**
■ Module Review **207**

Module 13 SPELLING

The Dictionary	**209**
Spelling Rules	**211**
Prefixes and Suffixes	**213**
Plurals of Nouns	**217**
Spelling Numbers	**220**
■ Module Review	**221**

MODULE 1: PARTS OF SPEECH

NOUNS

The Eight Parts of Speech			
noun	adjective	pronoun	conjunction
verb	adverb	preposition	interjection

1a A *noun* is a word used to name a person, place, thing, or idea.

Persons	carpenter, Ray Charles, sister, child
Places	canyon, Kenosha, neighborhood, basement
Things	desk, train, footprint, Pulitzer Prize, dog
Ideas	courage, happiness, truth, fairness, generosity

1b A *common noun* names a class of things. A *proper noun* names a particular person, place, or thing.

Common Nouns	Proper Nouns
planet, state, river	Venus, Idaho, Rio Grande
artist, president	Henri Matisse, Thomas Jefferson
monument, building	Vietnam Veterans Memorial, Empire State Building
ship, airplane	*Merrimack, Kitty Hawk*

1c *Concrete nouns* name an object that can be perceived by the senses. *Abstract nouns* name a quality or an idea.

Concrete Nouns	cat, moon, lightning, cotton, banana, George Washington, money, China, flower, book
Abstract Nouns	freedom, strength, gentleness, failure, love, anxiety, pride, hope, intelligence, honesty, admiration

EXERCISE 1 Identifying and Classifying Common and Proper Nouns

In each of the sentences below, underline the common nouns, and double underline the proper nouns.

EX. 1. A sari is a garment worn by women in India.

1. One book talked about the crash of the *Titanic* into an iceberg in the Atlantic.
2. Karen and Leon are coming to my house to watch the Super Bowl.
3. The surprise was four tickets to Hawaii.
4. Judge Miller decided that both men should pay for damages.
5. *Jahdu* is the name of the hero in a story by Virginia Hamilton.
6. Her attitude was pleasant, but her remarks were not.
7. Members of the Neighborhood Merchants Association met to nominate officers for the coming year.
8. *Calvin & Hobbes* was a cartoon strip distributed across the country.
9. *The Joy Luck Club,* a novel by Amy Tan, was made into a movie.
10. After leaving office, President James Madison spent his later years at Montpelier, his estate in Virginia.

EXERCISE 2 Identifying and Classifying Concrete and Abstract Nouns

In each of the sentences below, underline the concrete nouns, and double underline the abstract nouns.

EX. 1. Our dog loves the freedom of our large yard.

1. Harriet Tubman risked her safety to help runaway slaves.
2. Vincent van Gogh is the artist who painted *The Starry Night.*
3. James appreciated the patience and kindness shown by his teacher.
4. Ramona dreamed that she won the role in the movie and shared her fame and fortune with her family.
5. Edgar Allan Poe is considered a master of mystery and suspense.
6. The actress wept with joy and gratitude when she won a Tony Award.
7. Mrs. Baron refused to allow the noise to ruin her speech.
8. What contributed to the causes of the Vietnam War?
9. Sonia has gained an appreciation of music.
10. I appreciate the faith and trust that my parents have in me.

MODULE 1: PARTS OF SPEECH

COMPOUND NOUNS

1d ***Compound nouns*** **are made up of two or more words put together to form a single noun. Some compound nouns are written as one word, some as two or more words, and some with hyphens.**

One Word	lighthouse, lifetime, clothespin
Two or More Words	Cape Cod, Mr. Li, tug of war
Hyphenated Word	son-in-law, forty-eight, runner-up

NOTE When you are not sure how to write a compound noun, look in a dictionary.

EXERCISE 3 Identifying Compound Nouns in Sentences

Underline the compound nouns in the sentences below.

EX. 1. Good friends can help build a person's self-esteem and self-confidence.

1. This restaurant has the best egg rolls in New London.
2. Mr. Thomasino, who teaches Spanish at the high school, also coaches football.
3. Zhai said that the annual Moon Festival is an important holiday in China.
4. Tammy was appointed spokesperson for the group.
5. The Sproutful Seed Company, which is located downtown, employs eighty-five workers.
6. The star of the city ballet is the daughter of a famous playwright.
7. Mom got tickets to the Book and Author Luncheon this afternoon.
8. The police officer stayed with the lost child until the child's grandmother came.
9. Cleon was away over the weekend, so he recorded some of his favorite programs on his DVR.
10. The nurse measured the man's blood pressure and took his temperature before bringing his food.

EXERCISE 4 Identifying Compound Nouns in a Paragraph

Underline the compound nouns in the paragraph below.

EX. [1] Dad told me about a thrilling moment in baseball.

[1] That moment came in the eighth inning of the first game of the 1954 World Series. [2] Thousands of excited fans crowded the stands of the Polo Grounds in New York City to watch New York battle Cleveland. [3] The level of excitement increased when Vic Wertz, the first batter in the lineup, stepped up to home plate. [4] The first baseman swung hard, sending the ball into the outfield. [5] The hopes of the Cleveland fans soared like skyrockets. [6] Surely this blast would bring in two base runners. [7] The fans' confidence was crushed, however, when the center fielder for New York made a spectacular catch. [8] Willie Mays quieted the cheers of those fans as he caught the ball and spun around. [9] With the talent and skill that had made him famous, he hurled the ball to the infield. [10] It was the game of a lifetime.

MODULE 1: PARTS OF SPEECH

PRONOUNS

1e A *pronoun* is a word used in place of a noun or more than one noun.

Personal Pronouns	I, me, my, mine, we, us, our, ours, you, your, yours, he, him, his, she, her, hers, it, its, they, them, their, theirs
Relative Pronouns	who, whom, whose, which, that
Interrogative Pronouns	who, whose, what, whom, which
Demonstrative Pronouns	this, that, these, those
Indefinite Pronouns	all, another, any, anybody, anyone, anything, both, each, either, everybody, everyone, everything, few, many, more, most, much, neither, nobody, none, no one, one, other, several, some, somebody, someone, something, such
Reflexive Pronouns	myself, ourselves, yourself, yourselves, himself, herself, itself, themselves

NOTE Pronouns such as *my, your, his, her, ours*, and *their* are considered possessive pronouns in this book, rather than adjectives. Follow your teacher's instructions in referring to such words.

A word that a pronoun stands for is called its ***antecedent.*** A pronoun may appear in the same sentence as its antecedent or in a following sentence.

EXAMPLE Pauli enjoyed making yogurt for **his** friends. **He** was glad that **they** enjoyed **it.** [*Pauli* is the antecedent of *his* and is in the same sentence as *his.* In the following sentence, *Pauli* is the antecedent of *He, friends* is the antecedent of *they*, and *yogurt* is the antecedent of *it.*]

EXERCISE 5 Identifying Pronouns

Underline the pronouns in the sentences below.

EX. 1. I asked Frank to bring in the mail when he came inside.

1. He kept two letters for himself and handed me a large envelope.

2. It was from a friend of mine in Colorado.

3. The envelope had seven stamps on the outside, and each was different from the others.
4. Looking at them was like looking at a mini-history lesson.
5. Among the stamps was one with a picture of Harriet Quimby on its face.
6. She was a female pilot who was also a pioneer in the history of aviation.
7. Another had a picture of Margaret Mitchell, who, I recall, wrote the novel *Gone with the Wind.*
8. Everyone knows her book was made into a movie.
9. Who is the man pictured on the stamp next to hers?
10. That is Luis Muñoz Marín, who served four terms as governor of Puerto Rico and greatly influenced its history.

EXERCISE 6 Identifying Pronouns and Their Antecedents

Underline the pronouns in the paragraph below. Double underline the antecedent of each pronoun.

EX. [1] The basket maker fanned herself with her fan.

[1] In Charleston, South Carolina, the basket makers visit among themselves as they sit, weaving their baskets. [2] The basket makers practice an art that is hundreds of years old. [3] It has been passed from one generation of women to another. [4] The baskets themselves were once made to store rice harvested by enslaved Africans. [5] Later, they were used to carry vegetables and fruit. [6] People who stop to watch a basket being made understand the skill and labor that basket weaving takes. [7] Even the smallest basket requires hours of work, making it expensive. [8] Tourists seem willing to pay the price without complaining about it. [9] They appreciate the fine workmanship. [10] The families who make baskets today are proud of their tradition.

MODULE 1: PARTS OF SPEECH

ADJECTIVES

1f An *adjective* is a word used to modify a noun or pronoun.

Adjectives make the meaning of a noun or a pronoun more definite. Words used in this way are called ***modifiers.*** An adjective may modify a noun or pronoun by telling *what kind, which one*, or *how many.*

What kind?	**red** paint, **new** friend, **light** rain
Which one?	**this** room, **those** books, **that** car
How many?	**five** feet, **ten** musicians, **many** hours

An adjective may be separated from the word it modifies by other words.

EXAMPLE The salad was **delicious.**

The most frequently used adjectives are *a, an*, and *the.* These words are usually called ***articles.***

A and *an* are ***indefinite articles.*** They indicate that a noun refers to one of a general group. *A* is used before words beginning with a consonant sound; *an* is used before words beginning with a vowel sound. *An* is also used before words beginning with the consonant *h* when the *h* is not pronounced.

EXAMPLES **A** car pulled up beside us.
Have you ever seen such **an** unusual painting?
Parsley is **an** herb.

The is the only ***definite article.*** It indicates that a noun refers to someone or something in particular.

EXAMPLE **The** chorus sang **the** song cheerfully.

EXERCISE 7 Identifying Adjectives in Sentences

Underline the adjectives in each of the following sentences, and double underline the word each adjective modifies. Do not include *a, an*, or *the.*

EX. 1. A blast of cold wind came through the open door.

1. The small plane made several attempts to land safely.
2. What lucky fishing group caught those trout?
3. Gertrude has developed an interesting and successful plan to save money.

4. Ancient glaciers have created a large wilderness in northern Labrador.
5. The fox dashed across the grassy meadow, looking for some food.
6. The prizewinning photographer said that his best shots were unusual.
7. Seven generations of my family have lived in the isolated village along the Pecos River in New Mexico.
8. The tired tourists walked around the foggy capital, but they did not complain about the bad weather.
9. The audience was surprised when ten members of the cast flew on invisible wires around the theater.
10. That castle in the Czech Republic is famous for its mahogany walls and stained-glass windows.

EXERCISE 8 Identifying Adjectives in Sentences

Draw a line under each adjective in the sentences below. Above it, write *indef.* for *indefinite article, def.* for *definite article*, or *adj.* for *adjective.*

EX. 1. We are going to New England to see the (*def.*) spectacular (*adj.*) fall (*adj.*) foliage.

1. If you want to see the best show of fall colors, travel to New England.
2. Only a few places in the world present this incredible spectacle.
3. Japan is one, along with New England, the mid-Atlantic states, and the Appalachian Mountains.
4. These places have the ideal combination of climate and native trees.
5. During the summer, certain trees make yellow colors in their leaves.
6. These remain hidden by the green chlorophyll in the leaves.
7. When fall comes and the chlorophyll disappears, the hidden yellows are revealed.
8. A tree may change sugar and other substances into vivid red chemicals.
9. This process seems magical.
10. A wet summer tends to result in a more beautiful fall show of leaves, which you should see.

MODULE 1: PARTS OF SPEECH

PRONOUNS AND NOUNS USED AS ADJECTIVES

1g Some words may be used either as adjectives or as pronouns.

To tell adjectives and pronouns apart, keep in mind what they do. Adjectives *modify* nouns; pronouns *take the place of* nouns. If a word is used as an adjective, a noun must closely follow it.

Adjective	Pronoun
These shoes are tight.	**These** are tight shoes.
Will **some** people not approve?	Will **some** not approve?
I'd like **that** book.	I'd like **that.**

1h Some words may be used either as nouns or as adjectives.

When a noun is used as an adjective, call it an adjective. Proper nouns used as adjectives are called ***proper adjectives.***

Common Nouns	Common Nouns Used as Adjectives
cheese	**cheese** omelet
city	**city** streets
silver	**silver** bracelet
Proper Nouns	**Proper Nouns Used as Adjectives**
Japanese	**Japanese** language
Malaysia	**Malaysian** economy
Beethoven	**Beethoven** symphony

EXERCISE 9 Identifying Nouns, Pronouns, and Adjectives

Classify each italicized word in the following paragraph. Above the word write *n.* for *noun, pron.* for *pronoun,* or *adj.* for *adjective.*

adj. *pron.*

EX. [1] A *New York City* vacation is *one* your family will always remember.

[1] *New York City* has so *much* to see and do that you will be busy from the moment you arrive. [2] When my family and *I* visited the *Big Apple* last summer, we stayed at.

[3] Our rooms were on the *seventh* floor, overlooking *Central Park.* [4] What an *ideal* place *that* is to watch people! [5] On *Monday* morning, we got up early and took a *subway* train to *Battery Park.* [6] There we purchased tickets for a *ferry* ride to the Statue of Liberty and *Ellis Island.* [7] The *copper* statue was awesome and rather frightening because of its huge *size.* [8] The *Ellis Island* portion of the trip reminded me that *America* is a land of *immigrants.* [9] Photographs of *some* of the twelve *million* people that passed through Ellis Island are displayed in its main building, *which* was recently renovated. [10] Later *that* day, we went over to *Manhattan* for dinner.

EXERCISE 10 Revising Sentences by Using Appropriate Adjectives

Add a variety of adjectives to make two entirely different sentences from each sentence below. Rewrite the sentences on your own paper.

EX. 1. With a smile, the boy greeted the dog.
1. *With a wide smile, the friendly boy greeted the dog.*
1. *With a timid smile, the boy greeted the yapping dog.*

1. The clouds hung over the city for days.
2. As guests began to arrive, the host spoke to the staff.
3. Under the porch was a chest stuffed with jewelry and coins.
4. Cora traveled on the bus to her job in the city.
5. The teacher gave a presentation to the students.
6. As Coco put the dishes on the table, Tim prepared a salad.
7. That author tells stories about people.
8. The people waited on the platform for the train to arrive.
9. The man who entered the room wore a mask and a coat.
10. Using a tool, the mechanic fixed the car.
11. The river flowed under the bridge.
12. When the cat leaped, the audience gasped.
13. Take the coat to the child.
14. We sat around the fire, telling stories.
15. Those apples aren't for eating, but these melons are.

MODULE 1: PARTS OF SPEECH

REVIEW EXERCISE

A. Identifying Nouns, Pronouns, and Adjectives

On the line before each sentence below, identify the italicized words by writing *n.* for *noun, pron.* for *pronoun*, or *adj.* for *adjective.* Underline the word each adjective modifies.

EX. _adj.; n._ 1. Those are *my* cousins from *Florida.*

_____ 1. Floridians enjoy a *warm* climate for most of the *year.*

_____ 2. Although the *thought* of warm weather is appealing, *I* am not sure *I* would like to deal with giant insects.

_____ 3. *Florida* officials have reported seeing *huge* grasshoppers.

_____ 4. *Who* told you about *this*?

_____ 5. I read about the *five-inch* grasshoppers in *a* magazine.

_____ 6. At *the* time, only *five* had actually been seen.

_____ 7. *These* creatures are native to places like *Costa Rica* and Brazil.

_____ 8. Hungry grasshoppers can eat a tremendous *amount* of *sugar cane.*

_____ 9. Because of *this* appetite, state officials expressed *concern.*

_____ 10. The *sugar cane* crop is *important* to the area's agricultural industry.

B. Identifying Nouns, Pronouns, and Adjectives

Underline each noun, pronoun, and adjective in the following sentences. In the space above each underlined word, classify the word by writing *n.* for *noun, pron.* for *pronoun*, or *adj.* for *adjective.* Double underline the word each adjective modifies. Do not include the articles *a, an,* or *the.*

n. *pron.* *n.* *adj.* *n.*

EX. 1. The voyage took them from Japan to the California coast.

1. The newborn chicken ate its first meal eight hours after it hatched.

2. The dealer purchased the Monet painting for an anonymous collector.

3. Aviva felt great satisfaction as she accepted the first-place award.

4. The bald eagle is a symbol of freedom for many United States citizens.

5. A visual illusion can make you believe you are seeing an object even though it is not there.

6. The ancient Mayan cities of El Mirador and Tikal are protected areas.

7. The pretty tune that she is humming is a Brahms lullaby.

8. Whenever I have to speak in front of a crowd, anxiety sets in.

9. Thea enjoys stand-up comics, and Bill Cosby is one of her favorites.

10. Because of their generosity and kindness to the community, the new library was named for the Lopezes.

C. Working Cooperatively to Write a Travel Advertisement

Work with a partner to create a travel brochure for a Caribbean vacation.

1. Choose an island in the Caribbean. Gather specific information about the island. You will probably want to learn about the climate, the beaches, the local culture, and the most popular tourist attractions and activities. On your own paper, make notes on your research.

EX. **JAMAICA**

an island in the Greater Antilles in the West Indies
named Xaymaca by Arawak Indians; name means "island of springs"
tropical climate with refreshing ocean winds
temperatures along the coast between 80° and 86°
beautiful sandy beaches
places to see: Montego Bay, Ocho Rios
things to do: snorkeling, scuba diving, exploring, sailing

2. Organize your notes. Work together to decide on the most appealing way to present the information. Then create a travel brochure of at least ten sentences, using a variety of nouns, pronouns, and adjectives. When you have finished, underline each noun, pronoun, and adjective. Above the words, write *n.* for *noun, pron.* for *pronoun*, and *adj.* for *adjective.* Do not label the articles *a, an*, and *the.*

n.
JAMAICA

pron. n. adj. adj. n. pron.
EX. *Forget your troubles. Let tropical Jamaican breezes whisk them away.*

MODULE 1: PARTS OF SPEECH

VERBS

1i A *verb* is a word that expresses action or a state of being.

Words such as *take, speak, run,* and *drive* are **action verbs.** Some action verbs express actions that cannot be seen—for example, *think, trust, recognize,* and *remember.*

EXAMPLES She **lifted** the box.
Should we value your judgment?

1j A *transitive verb* expresses an action directed toward a person or a thing named in the sentence.

EXAMPLES Mark **hugged** his parents. [The action of the verb *hugged* is directed toward *parents.*]
Does Sheilah **write** poetry? [The action of the verb *writes* is directed toward *poetry.*]

1k An *intransitive verb* expresses action or a state of being without referring to an object.

EXAMPLES The crowd **cheered.**
The plane **landed** on the runway.

The same verb may be transitive in one sentence and intransitive in another. An intransitive verb is often used when the emphasis is on the action rather than on the person or thing affected by it.

EXAMPLES Carrie **waved** her arm. [transitive]
Carrie **waved** quickly. [intransitive]

EXERCISE 11 Identifying Action Verbs

Underline the verb in each sentence below.

EX. 1. Rudy raked the leaves in the back yard.

1. A cold wind whipped through the trees.
2. Mary expects an important letter in the mail.
3. Because of the drought, the farmer worried about his vegetable crop.
4. Mrs. Tsao poured hot Chinese tea from the porcelain teapot.
5. Coreen recited the poem aloud for the class.

EXERCISE 12 Identifying Transitive and Intransitive Verbs

In the sentences below, identify each italicized verb as transitive or intransitive. Write *trans.* for *transitive* or *intr.* for *intransitive* on the line before each sentence.

EX. 1. ___*intr.*___ Robert *arrived* late.

_______ 1. That rude remark *irritated* her.

_______ 2. The squirrel *jumped* from the tree branch onto the bird feeder.

_______ 3. When the commotion started, *did* Bill *walk* out?

_______ 4. She *analyzed* the relationship of the two main characters.

_______ 5. The cats *sat* silently and watched the hawk soaring above them.

_______ 6. We listened while Mr. Siadat *read* the opening verses of the poem.

_______ 7. The English language *borrows* words from many cultures.

_______ 8. Buffalo no longer *roam* freely over the Great Plains.

_______ 9. Jo and Ina piled the necessary provisions into the canoe and *pushed* off.

_______ 10. The writer N. Scott Momaday *spent* a part of his youth on Apache, Pueblo, and Navajo reservations.

_______ 11. The lost explorers *wandered* aimlessly through the jungle.

_______ 12. Miguel gave a rousing campaign speech to the student body.

_______ 13. In chemistry class we *did* an experiment with sulfuric acid.

_______ 14. The teacher *turned* to me and said, "Did you do your homework?"

_______ 15. *Have* you *picked* a bushel of apples?

EXERCISE 13 Writing Sentences with Transitive and Intransitive Verbs

For each verb below, write two sentences on your own paper. In one sentence, use the verb as a transitive verb, and underline the person or thing the action is directed toward. In the other sentence, use the verb as an intransitive verb.

EX. 1. sang

1. *Denise sang the school song.* 1. *Denise sang sweetly.*

1. kept
2. taught
3. whispered
4. painted
5. climbed
6. moved
7. left
8. rested
9. learned
10. drove

LINKING VERBS

1l A *linking verb* links, or connects, the subject with a noun, a pronoun, or an adjective in the predicate. The verb *be* may express a state of being without having a complement.

A ***complement*** is a word or group of words that completes the meaning of a predicate.

The most commonly used linking verbs are forms of the verb *be*.

Forms of *Be*			
be	being	will be	shall be
am	can be	would be	should be
are	could be	have been	shall have been
is	may be	has been	should have been
was	might be	had been	will have been
were	must be	could have been	would have been

Other Commonly Used Linking Verbs			
appear	grow	seem	stay
become	look	smell	taste
feel	remain	sound	turn

EXAMPLES Lynda Sagor **is** my doctor. [Lynda Sagor = doctor]
Why **does** that **sound** familiar? [familiar that]
The flowers **smell** exotic. [exotic flowers]
Our dog **can** sometimes **be** a nuisance. [dog = nuisance]

Many linking verbs can be used as action (nonlinking) verbs as well.

EXAMPLES The tree **grew** tall. [linking verb: tall tree]
The tree **grew** several new branches. [action verb]

Even *be* is not always a linking verb. It may be followed by only an adverb. In the sentence *They are here*, the word *here* is an adverb. It does not refer to the subject, *They*. To be a linking verb, the verb must be followed by a noun, a pronoun, or an adjective that refers to the subject.

EXERCISE 14 Identifying Linking Verbs

Underline the linking verb in each sentence below. Then double underline the two words that each verb links.

EX. 1. The guitarist was pleased with the applause.

1. Marguerita feels peaceful after a long run.
2. The tacos on that platter smell delicious.
3. Virgil seemed anxious before class today.
4. Wanda's older brother is my math tutor.
5. That story became a myth among the Seneca people.
6. Good friends have always been important to me.
7. That was a childish prank.
8. The stone statues almost looked alive in the moonlight.
9. Gladys might someday become a dancer with a jazz troupe.
10. Does that story sound fishy to you?
11. That could have been Ronald up there.
12. You may be right, but I doubt it.
13. We were being too noisy.
14. I am sure you had it a moment ago.
15. My sister's green eyes gradually turned brown.

EXERCISE 15 Writing Sentences Using Verbs as Both Linking and Action Verbs

On your own paper, write two sentences for each of the verbs below. In the first sentence, use the verb as a linking verb. Underline the two words that the verb connects. In the second sentence, use the verb as an action verb.

EX. 1. become
1. *According to the rules, the person with the most points becomes the winner.*
1. *This straw hat becomes you.*

1. feel
2. sound
3. taste
4. grow
5. remain
6. appear
7. smell
8. stay
9. turn
10. look

VERB PHRASES

1m A *verb phrase* consists of the main verb and its *helping verbs* (also called *auxiliary verbs*).

Commonly Used Helping Verbs				
can	do	has	might	should
could	does	have	must	will
did	had	may	shall	would

The forms of the verb *be* are also helping verbs.

EXAMPLES **Would** Alfred **like** some help?
You **should have offered** sooner.
I **did** not **get** home until a few minutes ago.
We **shall** probably **be finished** in an hour.

NOTE The word *not* in a phrase such as *could not go* is not a helping verb. Both *not* and the contraction *–n't* are adverbs.

EXERCISE 16 Identifying Verb Phrases

Underline the verb phrase in each of the following sentences. Double underline the helping verbs in each verb phrase. One sentence contains two verb phrases.

EX. 1. *Miss Saigon* was performed at the Wang Center in Boston.

1. You may have heard of the youth workshops at the Wang Center.
2. During the run of *Miss Saigon*, hearing-impaired students from the Horace Mann School could participate in the Young at Arts program.
3. This program was established in 1988.
4. Thousands of young people have been introduced to the arts through these workshops.
5. How did the *Miss Saigon* workshops help the students?
6. The acting games may have increased their awareness of the Vietnam War.
7. Wasn't the story of *Miss Saigon* based on events in the Vietnam War?
8. Discussions with the cast and crew members before and after the play must have been enjoyable.

9. The Young at Arts program has also prepared study guides.
10. These guides should have stimulated students' interest in the play.
11. Did you ever see this popular play?
12. The Wang Center has served the entire community.
13. Will the theater be making changes to the entrances?
14. The center does offer performances that are interpreted in American Sign Language.
15. I have liked learning that language.

EXERCISE 17 Using Verb Phrases

Complete the sentences below by rewriting them on your own paper. Add helping verbs to the verbs in parentheses to create verb phrases.

EX. 1. I _______________ (*read*) a book about opera.
1. *I have been reading a book about opera.*

1. My aunt _______________ (*want*) to take me to the opera for a long time.
2. She _______________ (*tell*) me that I limit my musical experiences.
3. She _______________ (*know*) that I wasn't wild about attending the opera.
4. That _______________ (*be*) why she ordered the two tickets for *Carmen* without telling me.
5. I _______________ (*act*) nicer when she told me, but I never hide my feelings.
6. However, she _______________ (*pay*) for the tickets, and my conscience warned me to be more agreeable.
7. So I said I _______________ (*go*), but I dreaded it.
8. Well, I _______________ (*be*) the first person to admit it when I am wrong.
9. I _______________ (*expect*) to be miserable.
10. From the moment the curtain _______________ (*raise*), I was thrilled with the colorful costumes, the lively music, the characters, and the story.

MODULE 1: PARTS OF SPEECH

ADVERBS

1n An *adverb* is a word used to modify a verb, an adjective, or another adverb.

Adverbs modify by telling *how, when, where,* or *to what extent.*

How?	Sadie opened the package **very carefully.**
When?	The catalogs arrived **yesterday.**
Where?	Tonya and Webster came **inside.**
To what extent?	I **almost** forgot your birthday. She is **extremely** beautiful.

Just as adjectives modify nouns and pronouns, adverbs modify verbs. An adverb makes the meaning of the verb clearer and more definite.

EXAMPLES The dog was barking **outside.** [*where*]
The dog barked **today.** [*when*]
The dog barked **loudly.** [*how*]
The dog **always** barked. [*to what extent*]

EXERCISE 18 Identifying Adverbs and the Verbs They Modify

Underline the adverbs in each of the following sentences. Then double underline the verb each adverb modifies. A sentence may have more than one adverb.

EX. 1. The police searched everywhere for Heta's bracelet.

1. The first-graders willingly participated in the geography contest.
2. That map of the world was brilliantly painted.
3. Claudia spoke endlessly about her summer vacation.
4. You left your jacket here.
5. Tecumseh was a Shawnee leader who fought tirelessly to preserve his people's heritage and land.
6. Today the mail arrived early, something that is unusual.
7. You can completely depend on Liz because she always works hard.

8. Dr. Martin Luther King, Jr., firmly opposed the use of violence in the civil rights movement and often spoke against it.
9. Kathy and Lynette constantly try to outdo each other.
10. Granddad exercises frequently and eats well.
11. Don't wander aimlessly around the room.
12. Now we must reach a decision about a movie.
13. The librarian does not allow pens here.
14. Diego nearly lost his hat.
15. Fortunately, school ends early on Wednesday.

EXERCISE 19 Using Adverbs

Complete each sentence below by writing an appropriate adverb on the line provided. The word or phrase in parentheses tells you what information the adverb should give about the verb.

EX. 1. She patted the frightened dog ___gently___ (*how*).

1. Kwam dived into the lake's cold water _______________ (*how*) and swam _______________ (*where*).
2. Halona _______________ (*to what extent*) relives her experiences during the hurricane.
3. Cobb will change the flat tire _______________ (*when*), but he will complain _______________ (*to what extent*) about it.
4. Mai looked _______________ (*where*) and waved _______________ (*how*) when she spotted us.
5. The mechanics couldn't locate the necessary part _______________ (*where*), so they can't fix the car _______________ (*when*).
6. Michael speaks Spanish _______________ (*how*).
7. The bird sang _______________ (*to what extent*) _______________ (*where*).
8. Steve _______________ (*how*) imagined what it would feel like to win the marathon _______________ (*when*).
9. Ada May _______________ (*how*) described to everybody what happened _______________ (*where*).
10. Kito spoke _______________ (*to what extent*) and _______________ (*how*) about recycling.

ADVERBS MODIFYING ADJECTIVES AND OTHER ADVERBS

Adverbs may modify adjectives.

EXAMPLES It was a **breathtakingly** beautiful sunset. [The adverb *breathtakingly* modifies the adjective *beautiful*.]
Did you leave because of the **extremely** long line? [The adverb *extremely* modifies the adjective *long*.]

NOTE The most frequently used adverbs are *too, so*, and *very*. Try to avoid these overused words in your writing. Instead, think of more precise adverbs to make your meaning clearer.

Adverbs may modify other adverbs.

EXAMPLES She explained **quite** carefully. [The adverb *quite* modifies the adverb *carefully*, telling *how* carefully.]
They will leave **early** tomorrow. [The adverb *early* modifies the adverb *tomorrow*, telling *when* tomorrow.]

NOTE Many adverbs end in *–ly*. However, not all words ending in *–ly* are adverbs. For instance, the following words are adjectives: *homely, kindly, lovely, deadly.* To determine a word's part of speech, look at how the word is used in the sentence. Do not rely on spelling alone.

EXERCISE 20 Identifying Adverbs and the Adjectives They Modify

Underline the adverbs in each of the following sentences. Then double underline the adjective each adverb modifies.

EX. 1. Inez was especially kind to her young cousin.

1. After exercising at the gym, Patsy was thoroughly exhausted.
2. Neil expressed concern that the crowd might become quite wild.
3. His uncle was a truly generous individual.
4. Isn't this hot-and-sour soup especially spicy?
5. The highwire routine was clearly dangerous.
6. George Shortsleeve's surprisingly accurate predictions about the mayoral race won him points among the voters.
7. That is an extremely heavy box; please, be careful lifting it.

8. Our family spent the night in a barely adequate hotel.
9. Rather ominous clouds hovered on the horizon.
10. Lucia wrote a particularly thoughtful paper analyzing the poem composed by Maya Angelou.
11. Is Liang unusually polite when she is tired?
12. Bao and Cam were completely sure about the directions they gave us.
13. When I am on a boat, my face is rarely green.
14. The overly choosy batter watched the pitches fly by.
15. Turn off the burner if the milk is almost hot.

EXERCISE 21 Identifying Adverbs and the Adverbs They Modify

Underline the adverbs in each of the sentences below. Then draw an arrow from one adverb to the other adverb it modifies.

EX. 1. Sal spoke rather slowly.

1. Utina explained quite precisely what occurred at City Hall.
2. Lucas sailed his small boat into the harbor late yesterday.
3. Arlene leaned alarmingly far over the ledge.
4. The people on the bus complained extremely loudly about the delay.
5. I awoke somewhat early, which is unusual for me.
6. Those plants in the greenhouse look especially healthy.
7. I am going to the hospital almost daily.
8. Megan travels to Montana quite often, doesn't she?
9. Barry hardly ever sees puffins on the shore.
10. Increasingly often I am finding toads in the yard.
11. Did you run even faster than last time?
12. "I thank you most sincerely, Ma'am."
13. I told my story perfectly calmly.
14. He was breathing terribly hard when he reached the summit.
15. The host of the party was rather fashionably dressed.

MODULE 1: PARTS OF SPEECH

PREPOSITIONS

1o A *preposition* is a word that shows the relationship of a noun or a pronoun to some other word in the sentence.

In the examples below, notice how the prepositions show six different relationships between *city* and the verb *flew.*

EXAMPLES
We flew **over** the city.
We flew **toward** the city.
We flew **beyond** the city.
We flew **across** the city.
We flew **around** the city.
We flew **into** the city.

A preposition always introduces a *phrase.* The noun or pronoun that ends a prepositional phrase is the ***object of the preposition***. In the previous examples, the object of each preposition is *city.*

Commonly Used Prepositions				
aboard	before	by	like	through
about	behind	concerning	near	to
above	below	down	of	toward
across	beneath	during	off	under
after	beside	except	on	until
against	besides	for	onto	up
along	between	from	outside	upon
among	beyond	in	over	with
around	but (meaning *except*)	inside	past	within
at		into	since	without

Prepositions may also be compound.

Compound Prepositions		
according to	in addition to	instead of
because of	in front of	on account of
by means of	in spite of	prior to

NOTE Depending on its use in a sentence, the same word may be either an adverb or a preposition.

EXAMPLES
Vince walked **inside.** [adverb]
Vince walked **inside** the house. [preposition]

EXERCISE 22 Using Prepositions

Write a preposition on each line to complete the sentences below.

EX. 1. Charlotte read a fictional story *about* the Civil War.

1. The weary soldiers marched slowly _______________ the field.
2. They had fought a mighty battle _______________ their country.
3. Many of their comrades had died _______________ yesterday's battle.
4. These remaining soldiers were grateful _______________ their survival.
5. Many of them had not eaten _______________ several days.
6. Several stopped to rest _______________ the large rocks or tree stumps.
7. They considered their accomplishments _______________ their failures.
8. When they finally reached the farmhouse, the youngest _______________ them collapsed on the ground.
9. The farmers helped carry the boy _______________ the house.
10. They would feed the soldiers and give them a place to sleep _______________ the next morning.
11. When the sun came up, the young soldier was still _______________ any strength.
12. The rest _______________ the troop decided they could not wait for him.
13. His friends waved as they walked _______________ his window.
14. _______________ a few days, the young man was well enough to travel.
15. He told the farmers he had survived only _______________ their kindness.

EXERCISE 23 Writing Sentences with Prepositions and Adverbs

On your own paper, write two sentences for each of the words below. In the first sentence, use the word as a preposition, and underline the prepositional phrase. In the second sentence, use the word as an adverb, and double underline the word the adverb modifies.

EX. 1. before
1. *Don't eat anything before dinner.*
1. *I heard that story before.*

1. below	5. over	9. above
2. near	6. around	10. down
3. under	7. outside	
4. up	8. in	

MODULE 1: PARTS OF SPEECH

CONJUNCTIONS AND INTERJECTIONS

1p A *conjunction* is a word used to join words or groups of words.

Conjunctions that join equal parts of a sentence are called ***coordinating conjunctions.***

Coordinating Conjunctions						
and	but	for	nor	or	so	yet

EXAMPLES Yesterday, we went to a movie **and** a play.
Did you see the western **or** the comedy?
I wanted to see the play, **for** Hoa directed it.

Conjunctions that are used in pairs are called ***correlative conjunctions***. Like coordinating conjunctions, correlative conjunctions join equal parts of a sentence.

Correlative Conjunctions		
both … and	neither … nor	whether … or
either … or	not only … but also	

EXAMPLES **Neither** my mother **nor** my father would reveal the secret.
Both my aunt **and** my grandfather showed up unexpectedly.
Their presence **not only** pleased us **but also** gave away the surprise.

1q An *interjection* is a word that expresses emotion and has no grammatical relation to other words in the sentence.

An *interjection* is usually followed by an exclamation mark. An interjection that shows only mild emotion is set off from the sentence by a comma.

EXAMPLES **Yuck!** That tastes terrible.
If they aren't here soon, **well,** I don't know what I'll do.

EXERCISE 24 Identifying Coordinating and Correlative Conjunctions

Underline the conjunctions in the paragraph below. In the space above the word, write *coor.* for *coordinating conjunction* or *corr.* for *correlative conjunction.*

coor.
EX. [1] I enjoy art, but I am not sure I understand it.

[1] Whether you understand art or not, you will appreciate the work of Jacob Lawrence. [2] His paintings reflect not only his own life experiences but also the life experiences of many African American people. [3] The figures in paintings such as *Builders #1* often express a particular state of mind or an emotion. [4] Lawrence was born in 1917 in Atlantic City and grew up in Harlem. [5] There he developed his interest in and fascination with African American history. [6] He studied history at the YMCA in Harlem, for he wanted to learn more about his culture. [7] Today Jacob Lawrence is a celebrated American artist, but his first painting job was with the Works Progress Administration. [8] During the Great Depression, the WPA both created jobs for people and paid the workers. [9] Neither the WPA nor Lawrence himself could have predicted that his work would become so famous. [10] Among his most famous paintings are portraits of Frederick Douglass, Harriet Tubman, and John Brown.

EXERCISE 25 Using Interjections

On your own paper, write a sentence using each of the interjections below. When punctuating your sentences, use both commas and exclamation points.

EX. 1. ouch
1. *Ouch! That really hurt!*

1. ah
2. wow
3. great
4. yikes
5. incredible
6. no
7. terrific
8. yeah
9. fantastic
10. hey

MODULE 1: PARTS OF SPEECH

MODULE REVIEW

A. Determining the Parts of Speech of Words

In the paragraph below, identify the part of speech of each italicized word or expression. On the line before each sentence, write *n.* for *noun, adj.* for *adjective, pro.* for *pronoun, v.* for *verb, adv.* for *adverb*, *prep.* for *preposition, conj.* for *conjunction,* and *intj.* for *interjection.*

EX. [1] _adv.; n.__ We *gladly* attended the concert of the West African group Farafina at the *Sanders Theater*.

[1] ______________ We were *extremely fortunate* to attend Saturday night's performance. [2] ______________ *Farafina* is an African musical troupe *from* Burkina Faso. [3] ______________ Since *their* formation in 1977, the group *has continued* to compose, arrange, and perform music in the traditional manner of their country. [4] ______________ They plan to maintain this strong tie to tradition, *yet* they admit that they are always *open* to new influences. [5] ______________ Farafina has been *popular* in Europe *for* a long time because audiences understand the music. [6] ______________ *Oh,* how exciting the *performance* was! [7] ______________ *As* the audience settled *down,* the music began. [8] ______________ The soft, melodic tones of the reed flute *were* soon *joined* by the more exotic sounds of the balafon, an *African* xylophone. [9] ______________ Before the singing or the dancing began, several *different* kinds of African drums, the doumdou'ba, the bara, the tama, *and* the djembe, added their rhythmic sounds. [10] ______________ I learned the names of these ancient African instruments *after* the performance was *over*.

B. Writing Sentences Using Words as Different Parts of Speech

On your own paper, write a sentence, using each of the following words or phrases. Above the word or phrase, identify its part of speech. Write *n.* for *noun, adj.* for *adjective, pro.* for *pronoun, v.* for *verb, adv.* for *adverb, prep.* for *preposition, conj.* for *conjunction*, and *intj.* for *interjection.*

EX. 1. gold *adj.*
1. *Kay bought a gold bracelet.*

1. sounded
2. neither … nor
3. gently
4. will be going
5. in spite of
6. challenged
7. ugh
8. today
9. this
10. table
11. White House
12. smelled
13. frequently
14. her
15. climbed
16. or
17. eek
18. across
19. must have known
20. computer

C. Determining and Writing Parts of Speech

A sailor on a pirate ship brings his captain this message about buried treasure. He found the note under the floorboards of a deserted shack on an island in the Atlantic Ocean. Unfortunately, mice have nibbled holes in the paper. For each blank, supply one word that makes sense, and write its part of speech above the word.

adv.
EX. 1 *This note will lead you* <u>*directly*</u> *to the buried treasure.*

1 ______________*! If you've found this note you are a lucky person. When my*
2 *ship was about to sink, I* ______________ *a chest with valuable jewels and*
3 *bags of golden coins. I quickly jumped into the water* ______________
4 *somehow managed to pull the chest* ______________*. I have been alone on*
5 *this deserted island for* ______________ *weeks and have been able to survive*
6 *by eating* ______________*. But it's time to leave. I found a small boat hidden*
7 ______________ *the shack this morning. The chest is too heavy and big to*
8 *bring on the boat, so I am going to bury* ______________*. I'm leaving this*
9 *note in case I don't make it. At least someone will enjoy the treasure. I am*
10 *burying the chest* ______________ *the* ______________*.*

MODULE 2: THE SENTENCE

SENTENCES AND SENTENCE FRAGMENTS

2a A *sentence* is a group of words that contains a subject and a verb and expresses a complete thought.

To express a complete thought, a sentence must say something that makes sense by itself. A group of words that does not express a complete thought is a ***fragment***, or a piece of a sentence.

FRAGMENT	provides food and shelter for a variety of birds and other wildlife
SENTENCE	The marsh provides food and shelter for a variety of birds and other wildlife.
FRAGMENT	when we looked carefully
SENTENCE	When we looked carefully, we noticed a motionless bird standing among the reeds.

EXERCISE 1 Identifying Sentences and Fragments

On the line before each of the following groups of words, write *sent.* for *sentence* and *frag.* for *fragment.* Add correct capitalization and punctuation to the sentences.

EX. *sent.* 1. ~~s~~he jumped over the fence and vanished (S written above)

_______ 1. Shannon most enjoyed the music of the mariachi bands

_______ 2. Jorge added his name to the petition

_______ 3. Liona and another woman in my family

_______ 4. have been designed by I. M. Pei

_______ 5. I quickly put on my kneepads and helmet

_______ 6. chemistry is easier for me than biology was

_______ 7. the Chicano Family Center in Texas

_______ 8. those dogs are all trained as guide dogs

_______ 9. nodded and smiled without saying anything

_______ 10. several of the trucks at the tollbooth

_______ 11. people wanted to hear about her life as an artist

_______ 12. a deserted stretch of highway

_______ 13. crisp, green lettuce and a tomato

_______ 14. Vincent is both a drummer and a piano player

_______ 15. and after a while, each day

EXERCISE 2 Completing Sentences

Each group of words below is a fragment. To form complete sentences, add either a subject with modifiers or a verb with modifiers to each fragment.

EX. 1. Yes, _our friend Iman_ speaks Arabic fluently.

1. In the middle of the table stood ______________________________.
2. Only my oldest brother ______________________________.
3. ______________________________ is wearing a blue and gold sari.
4. My favorite breakfast food was ______________________________.
5. The flames of the eight candles ______________________________.
6. In July, the three-day fair ______________________________.
7. ______________________________ screeched to a halt in front of me.
8. ______________________________ showed a picture of one of the ancient gods.
9. ______________________________ asked who had painted this portrait.
10. Around his wrist was ______________________________.
11. As the fog slowly rose, shapes of houses ______________________________.
12. ______________________________ cooked slowly.
13. Our two cats and the dog ______________________________.
14. ______________________________ closed with a crash.
15. ______________________________ turned down the volume on the radio.
16. Included in the crafts fair were ______________________________.
17. Sculptors, painters, and photographers ______________________________.
18. Did ______________________________ jump up on the stage?
19. ______________________________ are admitted free of charge.
20. ______________________________ enjoy eating Indian food.

MODULE 2: THE SENTENCE

RUN-ON SENTENCES

2b A *run-on sentence* is two or more complete sentences that are written as one sentence.

The two kinds of run-on sentences are the fused sentence and the comma splice. In a ***fused sentence,*** the writer has joined two or more complete sentences, with no punctuation mark between them.

RUN-ON The heart of Amish country is Pennsylvania there you can see samples of beautiful Amish quilts.

CORRECT The heart of Amish country is Pennsylvania. There you can see samples of beautiful Amish quilts.

In a ***comma splice,*** the writer has joined two or more sentences using only a comma to separate them.

RUN-ON Amish quilts use unexpected combinations of bold colors, the results are striking.

CORRECT Amish quilts use unexpected combinations of bold colors. The results are striking.

There are several ways to revise a run-on sentence. You can always make two separate sentences. But you can also make a compound sentence if the independent clauses in the run-on are closely related.

(1) You can make a compound sentence by adding a comma and a coordinating conjunction (*and, but, nor, or,* or *yet*).

RUN-ON Food is scarce for birds in the winter you can help by feeding them.

REVISED Food is scarce for birds in the winter, but you can help by feeding them.

(2) You can make a compound sentence by adding a semicolon.

RUN-ON There are many types of bird feeders many of these you can make yourself.

REVISED There are many types of bird feeders; many of these you can make yourself.

(3) You can make a compound sentence by adding a semicolon and *conjunctive adverb*—a word such as *also, however, instead, meanwhile, nevertheless, still,* or *therefore.* A conjunctive adverb needs to be followed by a comma.

RUN-ON Hang your bird feeder where you can watch the birds, keep it out of the reach of cats.

REVISED Hang your bird feeder where you can watch the birds; however, keep it out of the reach of cats.

EXERCISE 3 Revising Run-on Sentences

On your own paper, revise each run-on sentences. If the sentence is correct write *C.*

EX. 1. Tecumseh was a leader of the Shawnee group of Native Americans his name means "shooting star."

1. *Tecumseh was a leader of the Shawnee group of Native Americans. His name means "shooting star."*

1. Tecumseh was born around 1768 in what is now Ohio the Shawnee lived throughout the midwestern states.
2. His father was a leader he was killed when Tecumseh was a child.
3. Tecumseh's brother Cheeseekan taught him the ways of Shawnee warfare he also taught Tecumseh leadership and speaking skills.
4. Tecumseh wanted to unite all of the peoples of the Great Lakes region he advocated for peaceful resolution of conflicts.
5. He was recognized as a leader when he was young, he was only sixteen when he took part in his first battle.
6. Cheeseekan was killed in a battle, Tecumseh became chief.
7. Tecumseh hated the practice of torture he would not permit it when he was leader.
8. Tecumseh and another brother, Tenskwatawa, built a village for their people on the Tippecanoe River, people from many places came to live in the village.
9. Tecumseh traveled, organizing a league of Native Americans, while he was away, his village was destroyed in the Battle of Tippecanoe.
10. Because an American general burned the village, Tecumseh supported the British in the War of 1812 he was killed in that war.

MODULE 2: THE SENTENCE

SUBJECT AND PREDICATE

2c A sentence consists of two parts: the *subject* and the *predicate*.

The ***subject*** is the part that names the person or thing spoken about in the rest of the sentence. It may come at the beginning, the end, or even the middle of a sentence. The ***predicate*** is the part that says something about the subject.

	SUBJECT		PREDICATE
EXAMPLES	The pioneers		crossed the desert at night.
	PREDICATE		SUBJECT
	Long and hard was		the journey.
	PREDICATE	SUBJECT	PREDICATE
	Have	you	read the women's diaries?

In these examples, the words labeled *subject* make up the ***complete subject***. The words labeled *predicate* make up the ***complete predicate***. Notice in the third example that parts of the complete predicate can come before and after the subject.

EXERCISE 4 Identifying the Complete Subject of a Sentence

Underline the complete subject in each sentence below. Remember that the subject may come at the beginning, the end, or even the middle of a sentence.

EX. 1. Many Japanese children own Daruma dolls.

1. Did Grandma own a cornhusk doll?
2. How interesting and colorful that book on dolls is!
3. Is the wooden doll still your favorite?
4. Rare and expensive is that doll in the picture.
5. My classmate Tony owns several kachina dolls.
6. Did that old rag doll belong to a family member?
7. Would you buy an antique doll?
8. The doll on the lower shelf is more than two hundred years old.
9. Was papier mâché ever used for a doll's head?
10. These wooden dolls were used in special ceremonies.

EXERCISE 5 Identifying Complete Subjects and Predicates

In each sentence below, underline the complete subject once and the complete predicate twice.

EX. 1. The cyclists planned a two-day journey.

1. A good bike trail simplifies travel.
2. Cool and crisp was the weather.
3. The tour leader will check the equipment of each bicycle.
4. Do you wear your helmet at all times?
5. Did Mavis adjust the bicycle seat and handlebars properly?
6. A ten-speed bike is nice, but not necessary, on long trips.
7. Each person carried a small tool kit and some foul-weather gear.
8. The plastic bottle on my bike holds one liter of water.
9. You have to use hand signals and follow safety regulations.
10. For most of our trip, we traveled along country roads.
11. The reds and yellows of the fall foliage glistened in the sunlight.
12. Apples, pumpkins, and vegetables were for sale at farm stores.
13. One roadside store advertised pure cider pressed from fresh apples.
14. How could we resist a taste of that drink?
15. By Sunday evening, all the bikers were tired but happy.
16. My brother has many hobbies.
17. Last Saturday, Eric bought tomatoes at the outdoor market.
18. The woman in the front row is my aunt.
19. That lucky Bella won some beautiful prizes.
20. Mr. Daly, the art teacher, exhibited a variety of origamis that his students had made.
21. Even young children can make simple paper creations.
22. Did Felina hit a homerun?
23. Into the night roared the steam engine.
24. Our class voted on the motion for a community project.
25. Who wrote *Barrio Boy*?

MODULE 2: THE SENTENCE

THE SIMPLE SUBJECT AND THE SIMPLE PREDICATE

2d The *simple subject* is the main word or group of words in the complete subject that tells *whom* or *what* the sentence is about.

SENTENCE	The bear on the shelf was carved out of soapstone.
COMPLETE SUBJECT	The bear on the shelf
SIMPLE SUBJECT	bear

A compound noun is considered one noun and may therefore be used as a simple subject.

SENTENCE	The white polar bear was made by an Inupiat carver.
COMPLETE SUBJECT	The white polar bear
SIMPLE SUBJECT	polar bear

NOTE In this book, the term *subject* refers to the simple subject unless otherwise indicated.

EXERCISE 6 Identifying Simple Subjects

In each sentence below, underline the simple subject.

EX. 1. Gwendolyn Brooks is one of my favorite authors.

1. One unit in my literature book was about African American poets of the eighties and nineties.
2. The boy in front of me read one poem with great feeling.
3. Another student in my class enjoys the poetry of Sonia Sanchez.
4. Next Friday evening a poet is speaking at our local bookstore.
5. Everyone in the class turned to the last stanza of the poem.
6. A number of the poems were about real people, including Dr. Martin Luther King, Jr., and Malcolm X.
7. The United States Poet Laureate is appointed annually by the Librarian of Congress.
8. The title of that poem is a single word.
9. Our local bookstore has an excellent selection of poetry books.
10. The anthology on the table looks like a reprint of one that was published in 2001.

2e The *simple predicate*, or *verb*, is the main word or group of words in the complete predicate.

SENTENCE	The bus lurched around a sharp bend in the road.
COMPLETE PREDICATE	lurched around a sharp bend in the road
SIMPLE PREDICATE	lurched

The simple predicate may be a single verb or a ***verb phrase*** (a verb and one or more helping verbs). When you identify the simple predicate, be sure to find all parts of the verb phrase.

SENTENCE	Have you found a pen?
COMPLETE PREDICATE	have found a pen
SIMPLE PREDICATE	have found
SENTENCE	I must have lost it here.
COMPLETE PREDICATE	must have lost it here
SIMPLE PREDICATE	must have lost

EXERCISE 7 Identifying Complete Predicates and Simple Predicates in Sentences

In each sentence in the paragraph below, underline the complete predicate once and the verb, or simple predicate, twice. Be sure to include all parts of a verb phrase.

EX. [1] People around the world will celebrate the harvest in various ways.

[1] Here in Chicago, we sit down for a big Thanksgiving dinner. [2] People in the Congo, though, hold a big hope of harvest festival. [3] They believe in the festival's guarantee of a good harvest. [4] Dancers and a drummer perform an elaborate circular dance for this festival. [5] Other people in Africa may schedule their harvest festivals during or after a harvest. [6] For example, the farmers in Ghana have a yam festival each August. [7] This festival may continue for up to two weeks. [8] I have also read about similar festivals in Myanmar, Syria, and many other countries. [9] The similarities among the festivals should not surprise you. [10] After all, every nation on earth wants to have enough food for its people.

MODULE 2: THE SENTENCE

FINDING THE SUBJECT

Finding the subject of a sentence is easier if you pick out the verb first. Then ask "Who?" or "What?" followed by the verb.

EXAMPLES A woman on my street **received** an award for heroism. [Who *received*? *A woman on my street* received. Therefore, *woman* is the subject.]
Beside the woman and her family **sits** the mayor. [Who *sits*? *The mayor* sits; *mayor* is the subject.]

2f The subject is never in a prepositional phrase.

EXAMPLE Two of my friends started a band. [Who started a band? *Two* started it, not *friends*, which is part of the prepositional phrase *of my friends*.]

2g In most questions, the subject follows the verb or helping verb.

Questions usually begin with a verb, a helping verb, or a word such as *what, when, where, how*, or *why*. One way to find the subject of a question is to turn the question into a statement and find the verb. Then ask "Who?" or "What?" in front of the verb.

EXAMPLES When will someone announce the winners?
Someone will announce the winners. [The question is turned into a statement. The subject is *Someone*.]

2h The word *there* or *here* may begin a sentence, but it is usually not the subject. *There* or *here* may be used as expletives or as adverbs telling where.

EXPLETIVE There is a **letter** for you. [What is for you? *Letter*. Therefore, *letter* is the subject. *There* doesn't add any meaning.]

ADVERB Here are your **tickets**. [What are here? *Tickets*.]

2i In requests and commands, the subject is usually not stated. In such a sentence, *you* is the understood subject. If the sentence includes a person's name, the name is not the subject. The name is called *a noun of direct address*.

REQUESTS	(You) Please open the door.	(You) Please pass the milk.
COMMANDS	(You) Help me, Tyler.	(You) Come here, Sam.

EXERCISE 8 Identifying Subjects and Verbs

In each sentence in the paragraph below, underline the subject once and the verb twice.

EX. [1] On the postcard is a picture of Nellie Cashman.

[1] As a teenager, Nellie Cashman came to the United States. [2] From Ireland to San Francisco she traveled. [3] In 1877, this woman traveled to Alaska with a group of gold miners. [4] There, Nellie looked for gold. [5] In addition, she ran a boardinghouse for other miners. [6] During the fall, a dangerous illness hit the camps. [7] This disease, scurvy, can be deadly. [8] People with scurvy must have fresh produce or some other source of Vitamin C. [9] Despite the freezing cold, Nellie, with six others, traveled to Victoria and back. [10] With her came almost a ton of lifesaving vegetables.

EXERCISE 9 Identifying Subjects and Verbs

In each sentence below, underline the subject once and the verb twice. If the subject is understood, write (*You*) on the line before the sentence.

EX. (*You*) 1. Look in the nutrition book on the top shelf.

_______ 1. Does orange juice have many vitamins?

_______ 2. Eat fresh fruits and vegetables whenever possible.

_______ 3. Look at all the jars in the canning cupboard of this old house.

_______ 4. How can someone store apples for a long time?

_______ 5. Your home freezer should keep foods at 0°F for best results.

_______ 6. There isn't enough space in the freezer for those peaches.

_______ 7. Here is a jar of homemade pickles for our picnic.

_______ 8. Why does that log cabin have a root cellar?

_______ 9. Put the milk in the coldest part of the refrigerator.

_______ 10. There is no way for us to finish this assignment by today.

MODULE 2: THE SENTENCE

COMPOUND SUBJECTS AND COMPOUND VERBS

2j A *compound subject* consists of two or more subjects that are joined by a conjunction and have the same verb. The conjunctions most often used to link the parts of a compound subject are *and* and *or*.

EXAMPLES **Mr. Pong** and the **clerk** shook hands. [Who shook hands? *Mr. Pong* and the *clerk*.]

Mr. Pong or the **clerk** will help you. [Again, the two parts of the compound subject are *Mr. Pong* and *clerk*.]

2k A *compound verb* consists of two or more verbs that are joined by a conjunction and have the same subject.

EXAMPLES On Tuesday I **brought** my history book home and **studied** module four.

Josh **called** but **did** not **leave** a message.

(You) **Come** inside and **have** dinner.

NOTE If the helping verb is the same for the two verbs in a compound verb, it may or may not be repeated. Both the subject and the verb may be compound.

EXAMPLE **Rosa** and **Pang will meet** you and **show** you around.

EXERCISE 10 Identifying Compound Subjects and Compound Verbs

In each of the following sentences, underline the subject once and the verb twice. If the subject is understood, write (*You*) on the line before the sentence.

EX. (*You*) 1. Visit a market and buy some handcrafts.

_______ 1. My sister and I shopped at several different Friendship Stores.

_______ 2. Some Chinese stores display and sell everything from herbal medicines to television sets and cameras.

_______ 3. Beijing and Shanghai attract numerous visitors every year.

_______ 4. At free markets many farmers buy and sell both handcrafts and foods.

_______ 5. Shop carefully and compare prices for any expensive purchases.

_______ 6. In Tianjin you and I can buy beautiful carpets or lovely glass.

_______ 7. My friend Tamala wanted a silk blouse but could not find the right color.

_______ 8. Eric and I looked at a sandalwood fan but bought a silk one instead.

_______ 9. Some stores can wrap your purchases and mail them anywhere in the world.

______ 10. After dinner my uncle or I will call and make plans for Friday and Saturday evening.

EXERCISE 11 Writing Compound Subjects and Verbs

Complete each sentence below by writing either compound subjects or compound verbs in the blanks. You also may add any necessary modifiers.

EX. 1. Next Friday ___*Tina*___ and ___*I*___ will make dinner.

1. Adrienne ____________________ the letter and ________________________ it.
2. ________________________ and __________________________ do not fly.
3. Before your first class, ___________________ and ___________________ will tell you about the cost of safety equipment.
4. In ten minutes, ______________________________________ the potatoes and ____ them.
5. You may ____________________ a tuxedo or ______________________ one.
6. ___________ or ___________will take your temperature and your blood pressure.
7. The vaccum cleaner _________________ and then ____________________.
8. After a long wait, the music finally ____________________________ but then ____.
9. Did ______________ or ______________ ever visit that new Mexican restaurant?
10. An eagle ______________ over the mountaintops and then ____ without warning.

MODULE 2: THE SENTENCE

COMPLEMENTS

21 A *complement* is a word or group of words that completes the meaning of a predicate.

A group of words may have a subject and a verb and still not express a complete thought.

INCOMPLETE	This picture looks	The batter hit
COMPLETE	This picture looks original.	The batter hit the ball.

Complements are never in prepositional phrases.

EXAMPLES Carlos wrote the **poem.** [*Poem* is the complement.]
Carlos thought about the poem. [*Poem* is part of the prepositional phrase *about the poem.*]

An adverb modifying a verb is not a complement. Only nouns, pronouns, and adjectives are complements.

EXAMPLES The train arrived **late**. [*Late* is an adverb, not a complement.]
Rosa is **late**. [*Late*, an adjective, is a complement.]

A complement may be compound.

EXAMPLES The concert starred **Jaime** and **Liz.**
The weather was **cold** and **rainy.**

EXERCISE 12 Identifying Subjects, Verbs, and Complements.

In each of the following sentences, underline the subject once and the verb twice. Double underline the complement if there is one.

EX. [1] The first longhorns in Hawaii were gifts from a British seaman.

[1] These cattle must have looked strange among the eucalyptus trees. [2] A gift of horses from the United States arrived on the island about ten years after the cattle. [3] These herds of cattle and horses have been destructive to vegetation. [4] Also, some of the descendants of these cattle actually attacked people. [5] During the 1830s, King Kamehameha II sent to California for vaqueros. [6] Many of them were Mexican, American Indian, and Spanish cowboys. [7] The Hawaiian cowboys' name for themselves was *paniolos*. [8] These Hawaiian cowboys wore western outfits with

a Polynesian look. [9] Soon the paniolos learned the necessary skills. [10] In time, Hawaii, as many Western states, had cattle drives and rodeos.

EXERCISE 13 Writing Sentence Complements

For each group of words below, write a complement to form a complete sentence.

EX. 1. After assembly, Mr. Torres introduced *the next speaker*.

1. During dinner last night, Jess seemed ______________________________ .
2. About twenty years ago, my grandmother discovered ______________________________ .
3. The person who called wanted ______________________________ .
4. Over the summer, Seki painted ______________________________ .
5. At the dance, everyone looked ______________________________ and ______________________________ .
6. We postponed our trip because the weather seemed ______________________________ .
7. Using a new computer program, Carl created ______________________________ .
8. For our fund-raising auction, Mrs. Bluehouse donated ______________________________ .
9. First, the ballet troupe performed ______________________________ .
10. For months, engineers planned ______________________________ .

MODULE 2: THE SENTENCE

SUBJECT COMPLEMENTS

2m A *subject complement* is a noun, a pronoun, or an adjective that follows a linking verb. A subject complement identifies, describes, or explains the subject.

EXAMPLES Paloma is my **cousin**. [*Cousin* identifies *Paloma.*]
This cocoa smells **wonderful**! [*Wonderful* describes *cocoa.*]

(1) A *predicate nominative* is a noun or a pronoun in the predicate that identifies or renames the subject of a sentence or a clause.

EXAMPLES This tadpole will become a big **frog**. [The noun *frog* renames the subject *tadpole.*]
The captain could be **she**. [The pronoun *she* identifies the subject *captain.*]

(2) A *predicate adjective* is an adjective in the predicate that describes the subject of a sentence or a clause.

EXAMPLES Is she **talented** also? [The adjective *talented* describes the subject *she.*]
Let's leave because this band is too **loud**! [The adjective *loud* describes *band*, the subject of the clause.]

Subject complements may be compound.

EXAMPLE The soldiers looked **tired** and **dirty**.

NOTE The subject complement may come before the subject of a sentence or a clause.

EXAMPLES What a great **pilot** you are! [*Pilot* is a predicate nominative renaming the subject *you.*]
I noticed how **tall** Avi had grown. [*Tall* is a predicate adjective describing *Avi.*]

EXERCISE 14 Identifying Subject Complements

In each of the following sentences, underline the subject complement or complements.

EX. 1. The woman on the horse might be she.

1. Within a few hours, the night grew noticeably colder.
2. The poet Phillis Wheatley became a free woman only after the death of her owner.
3. This vegetable soup seems slightly thicker than the other soup does.
4. That unusual-looking aircraft was the winner of the last competition.

5. The main character in this story is a professional musician.
6. Despite fame, Arianna remained modest and friendly to everyone.
7. Are the sneakers in the window leather?
8. In 1993, writer Toni Morrison became the first African American winner of the Nobel Prize for literature.
9. That unplanned meeting seemed successful!
10. During the last hour of practice, your violin playing sounded really professional.

EXERCISE 15 Identifying Subjects, Verbs, and Subject Complements

For each sentence in the paragraph below, identify each subject, verb, and subject complement. In the space above the word, write *s.* for *subject, v.* for *verb, p.n.* for *predicate nominative*, or *p.a.* for *predicate adjective*.

s. *v.* *p.a.*
EX. 1. The rain forests of South America are unique.

[1] For years, the resources of the rain forests seemed unlimited. [2] After all, the area was large and isolated. [3] It did not remain isolated for long, however. [4] South American rain forests are rich sources of beautiful hardwoods. [5] Many of these woods are quite valuable to furniture makers and artists. [6] After years of harvesting these trees, the forests had become damaged. [7] Today, however, many landowners are more aware of the value of the forest itself. [8] Some parts will probably remain unspoiled national parks. [9] Other lands have become tree farms, where people plant trees as well as cut them. [10] With luck, these farms can survive and still become good sources of income for their owners.

MODULE 2: THE SENTENCE

OBJECTS

Objects are complements that do not refer to the subject. They follow action verbs rather than linking verbs.

2n A *direct object* is a noun or pronoun that directly receives the action of a verb or shows the result of the action. A direct object answers the question "What?" or "Whom?" after an action verb.

EXAMPLES The marchers carried the **petition** to the courthouse. [Carried *what*? *Petition.*]
Mrs. Washington asked **us** to wait. [Asked *whom*? *Us*.]

Verbs that express mental action, such as *study* and *understand*, are just as much action verbs as are verbs that express physical action, such as *climb* and *hit*.

EXAMPLE My brother **is studying art** in college. [Is studying *what*? *Art.*]

NOTE Direct objects are never found in prepositional phrases.

EXAMPLES Sarah wrote two **articles.** [*Articles* is the direct object.]
Sarah writes for our newspaper. [*Newspaper* is part of the prepositional phrase *for our newspaper*.]

2o An *indirect object* is a noun or pronoun that precedes the direct object and tells *to whom* or *for whom* (or *to what* or *for what*) the action of the verb is done.

DIRECT OBJECT Hisoka made **lunch.** [Made *what*? *Lunch.*]
INDIRECT OBJECT Hisoka made **us** lunch. [Made *lunch for whom? Us.*]

If the word *to* or *for* is used in the sentence, the noun or pronoun following it is part of a prepositional phrase, not an indirect object.

EXAMPLES Carlota gave **me** directions. [*Me* is the indirect object.]
Carlota gave directions **to me.** [*Me* is part of the prepositional phrase *to me.*]

Both direct and indirect objects may be compound.

EXAMPLE The clerk handed **Tonya** and **me** two **bags** and a **carton.**

EXERCISE 16 Identifying Verbs and Their Direct Objects

In the sentences below, underline the verb or verb phrase once. Underline each direct object twice.

EX. 1. As a child, Florence Sabin loved books.

1. Young Florence Sabin attended Smith College and Johns Hopkins Medical School.
2. The head of the anatomy department suggested a special project to her.
3. After graduation, Dr. Sabin studied the lymphatic system.
4. For more than twenty years, she taught students at Johns Hopkins.
5. Her work in the field of medicine saved many lives.

EXERCISE 17 Identifying Direct and Indirect Objects

In the sentences below, underline the direct objects once and any indirect objects twice. [Note: Not every sentence has an indirect object.]

EX. 1. Aziza is teaching them the song.

1. The man in the corner booth sold us wonderful homemade bread.
2. At the book sale, the ticket taker handed each shopper a paper bag.
3. Before practice, the coach read the class the safety rules.
4. The previous owner had built the treehouse for his children.
5. After a long silence, my pen pal finally wrote me a long, newsy letter about his new apartment.
6. For this job, you must give the doctor a completed health form.
7. In the last few seconds of the game, Flora tossed the ball to me.
8. My grandmother gave my father a photograph album from Cuba.
9. Before he left, Chim promised me a tennis lesson Thursday afternoon.
10. Slowly and carefully, I lifted the corner of the blanket.
11. Remember your chores, Mark.
12. My oldest sister plays tennis for her school.
13. In this movie, the pirate gives the little boy the map.
14. Is she teaching herself the new dance steps?
15. Clara wrote Ms. Ching a letter after our science fair.

MODULE 2: THE SENTENCE

CLASSIFYING SENTENCES BY PURPOSE

2p Sentences may be classified as *declarative, imperative, interrogative*, or *exclamatory*.

(1) A *declarative* sentence makes a statement. All declarative sentences are followed by periods.

EXAMPLES Two members of the road crew set up the amplifiers.
When Ray Charles sat down to play, the audience clapped wildly.

(2) An *imperative* sentence gives a command or makes a request. Imperative sentences usually end with periods, but strong commands may end with exclamation points.

EXAMPLES Please hold this. Watch my hands. Don't!

(3) An *interrogative* sentence asks a question. Interrogative sentences are followed by question marks.

EXAMPLES How much does this cost? Can you tie an obi?

(4) An *exclamatory* sentence expresses strong feeling. Exclamatory sentences are followed by exclamation points.

EXAMPLES What a display that was! How scared we were!

NOTE Any sentence may be spoken in such a way that it is exclamatory. In this case, it should be followed by an exclamation point.

EXAMPLES This is a disaster! [Declarative becomes exclamatory.]
Stop that noise! [Imperative becomes exclamatory.]
How about that! [Interrogative becomes exclamatory.]

EXERCISE 18 Identifying the Four Kinds of Sentences

On the line before each of the following sentences, identify the type of sentence. Write *dec.* for *declarative, imp.* for *imperative, inter.* for *interrogative*, or *excl.* for *exclamatory.*

EX. *inter.* 1. Is that Golda Meir?

_______ 1. Look at the article I found in this history magazine.

_______ 2. She was born in Russia and later moved to the United States with her parents.

_______ 3. How did she become prime minister of Israel?

_______ 4. What an interesting woman she was!

_______ 5. In 1948, she was Israel's representative to the Soviet Union.

_______ 6. What an unusual coincidence!

_______ 7. Didn't she retire from government office for a period of time?

_______ 8. Golda Meir served as prime minister of Israel for five years and then retired again.

_______ 9. Read *My Life*, her autobiography, and find out why she retired.

______ 10. Was Meir a prime minister at the same time as Indira Gandhi?

______ 11. Gandhi learned about politics at her father's side.

______ 12. When did she become prime minister of India?

______ 13. Tell me why she declared a state of emergency.

______ 14. How much power she had!

______ 15. She was out of the country for a few years.

EXERCISE 19 Working Cooperatively to Write T-shirt Slogans

You are a T-shirt designer who has been asked to create several designs and slogans for an ecology fair in your city. Work with a partner to write four different slogans, using each type of sentence once. Then classify your sentences by purpose. Write your slogans on the lines below.

EX. 1. *Have you hugged a green plant today? (interrogative)*

1. ______________________________

____

____

2. ______________________________

____

____

3. ______________________________

____

____

4. ______________________________

____

____

MODULE 2: THE SENTENCE

MODULE REVIEW

A. Understanding the Parts of a Sentence

On your own paper, define each of the terms below and give an example to illustrate it.

EX. 1. a fragment
A fragment is a group of words that isn't a complete sentence.
born in Paris in 1981 and died twenty years later

1. a sentence
2. a complete subject
3. a complete predicate
4. a simple subject
5. a simple predicate
6. a subject complement
7. a direct object
8. an indirect object
9. an understood subject
10. a predicate adjective

B. Identifying Subjects, Verbs, and Complements

On the line before each sentence, identify each of the italicized words. Write *s.* for *subject, v.* for *verb, p.a.* for *predicate adjective, p.n.* for *predicate nominative, d.o.* for *direct object*, or *i.o.* for *indirect object*.

EX. *s.; d.o.* 1. Do *you* like *tomatoes*?

_____ 1. For supper, Dad served *us* fresh *tomatoes* and *corn*.
_____ 2. *Both* of these foods were originally *natives* of Peru.
_____ 3. The ancient Incas *grew* a *number* of different tomatoes.
_____ 4. To the explorer Pizarro, the red *fruits* were *"love apples."*
_____ 5. As a cultivated crop, corn *may be* much *older* than tomatoes.
_____ 6. The ancient Incas *buried corn* with their dead.
_____ 7. The tomato *became* quite *popular* in Italy in the 1500s.
_____ 8. For years, many *people* actually *considered* tomatoes dangerous and sometimes even poisonous.
_____ 9. The *plants* were mainly *decorative* instead of useful.
_____ 10. Today people all over the world *eat* the *tomato* in a number of different forms.

C. Classifying Sentences by Purpose

Classify each sentence below. On the line before the sentence, write *dec.* for *declarative, inter.* for *interrogative, imp.* for *imperative, or excl.* for *exclamatory*. Then supply the proper end punctuation.

EX. ___*dec.*___ 1. Everyone in this room is related

_______ 1. What a wonderful idea Kessie had

_______ 2. When will you have your family reunion

_______ 3. We can hold it during the last week of August

_______ 4. What will the theme of the party be

_______ 5. Think of something that can include all four generations attending all the festivities

_______ 6. I have a great idea

_______ 7. Get a large piece of wrapping paper or shelf paper

_______ 8. What good will that do anyone

_______ 9. The older family members can name their relatives and the younger ones can draw a family tree

_____ 10. Marta, can you reproduce the finished product and give everyone a copy

D. Writing Sentences

On your own paper, write sentences according to each of the following guidelines. Underline the subject once and the verb twice in each sentence. If the subject is understood, write *(You)*.

EX. 1. a sentence with a predicate adjective
Your kimono is beautiful.

1. a sentence with an indirect object
2. an exclamatory sentence
3. a sentence with a compound verb
4. a sentence with a predicate adjective
5. a sentence with a compound subject
6. a sentence beginning with *Here*
7. a sentence with a direct object and no indirect object
8. an interrogative sentence
9. an imperative sentence
10. a declarative sentence with a verb phrase

MODULE 3: THE PHRASE

PREPOSITIONAL PHRASES

3a A *phrase* is a group of related words that is used as a single part of speech and does not contain both a verb and its subject.

EXAMPLES will be leaving [verb phrase; no subject]
after the World Series [prepositional phrase; no subject or verb]

3b A *prepositional phrase* is a group of words consisting of a preposition, a noun or pronoun that serves as the object of the preposition, and any modifiers of that object.

EXAMPLES Please be quiet during the next few **minutes.** [*Minutes* is the object of the preposition *during*. The adjectives *the, next*, and *few* modify *minutes*.]
Will you get the scissors for **me?** [*Me* is the object of the preposition *for*.]

A preposition may have a compound object.

EXAMPLES with **Sasha** and **her**
under the **tables** and **chairs**

EXERCISE 1 Identifying Prepositional Phrases

Underline all the prepositional phrases in the paragraph below.

EX. [1] Many African American soldiers helped fight the War <u>of 1812</u>.

[1] The War of 1812 was fought between Britain and the United States.

[2] During that war, African Americans fought in battles on land and on water.

[3] They saw action in battles on the Great Lakes and were especially successful fighting the Battle of Lake Erie. [4] Two African American battalions helped Andrew Jackson to win the Battle of New Orleans against the British. [5] Jackson later praised the African American soldiers for their patriotism, bravery, and enthusiasm.

EXERCISE 2 Identifying Prepositions and Their Objects

In the sentences below, underline each prepositional phrase, and draw brackets around the object of the preposition.

EX. 1. There are many lighthouses along the [coast] of [New England].

1. The rescuers searched the water from morning until night.
2. They were looking for a small boat with three teenagers on board.
3. The boat had been missing since the afternoon of the previous day.
4. With luck, they would find the teenagers safe and sound.
5. They found the boat overturned three miles from the shore.
6. At dusk they spotted one of the three teenagers.
7. He was clinging to a life preserver.
8. Using a cable and a net, the rescuers lifted him from the water and into a helicopter.
9. The teenager told the rescuers that his friends had swum toward a nearby lighthouse.
10. The lighthouse stood on a tiny island about a mile away.
11. The rescuers flew over the island.
12. They shined the helicopter's searchlights onto the beaches and rocks of the island.
13. One rescuer spotted two people lying on some rocks near the lighthouse.
14. The helicopter flew the three teenagers to a hospital, where they were treated for exposure and released.
15. After their treatment and release, the three teenagers thanked the rescue team at a meeting with reporters.

MODULE 3: THE PHRASE

ADJECTIVE PHRASES AND ADVERB PHRASES

3c A prepositional phrase that modifies a noun or a pronoun is an *adjective phrase.*

An adjective phrase follows the noun or pronoun that it modifies. Adjective phrases answer the same questions that adjectives answer: *What kind? Which one? How many?* and *How much?* An adjective phrase may also modify the object of another prepositional phrase.

EXAMPLES The little book **of poems** sold for ninety-five cents. [The phrase *of poems* modifies the noun *book.* It tells *what kind.*]

All **of the puppies** have been vaccinated. [The phrase *of the puppies* modifies the pronoun *all.* It tells *what kind.*]

The car will seat a group **of six or more.** [The phrase *of six or more* modifies the noun *group*. It tells *how many.*]

Some **of the books on the table** were marked "Half off." [The phrase *of the books* modifies the pronoun *some*. It tells *which ones. Books* is the object of the preposition *of.* The phrase *on the table* modifies *books*. It tells *which ones.*]

3d A prepositional phrase that modifies a verb, an adjective, or another adverb is an *adverb phrase.*

Adverb phrases tell *when, where, why, how,* or *to what extent*. They may come before or after the words they modify.

EXAMPLES The cougar climbed **up the rocks.** [The phrase *up the rocks* modifies the verb *climbed.* It tells *where.*]

The singers were very popular **with the audience.** [The adverb phrase *with the audience* modifies the adjective *popular.*]

The ball sailed far **over the fence.** [The phrase *over the fence* modifies the adverb *far*. It tells *to what extent.*]

More than one adverb phrase may modify the same word.

EXAMPLES **In the first act,** Sharon sang **with grace and ease.** [*In the first act* tells *when* Sharon sang, and *with grace and ease* tells *how* she sang.]

EXERCISE 3 Identifying Adjective Phrases

Underline all adjective phrases in the sentences below. Then draw an arrow from each phrase to the word or words it modifies. Some sentences may have more than one phrase.

EX. 1. The houses by the river were all flooded.

1. The scientist was studying communication among chimpanzees.
2. A duck slept under the bridge over the Colorado River.
3. No one in the troop noticed the elk with the big antlers.
4. A charango is a small Latin American guitar from the Andes.
5. A picture in the newspaper showed a man walking thirteen dogs.
6. The flowers along the edge of the lawn included hyacinths and irises.
7. A blanket of snow covered the sleepy little town.
8. The science museum contained a display of a woolly mammoth with large tusks.
9. An alleyway between two large buildings was the site of the street fair.
10. The postcard showed the Arc de Triomphe in Paris.

EXERCISE 4 Identifying Adverb Phrases and the Words They Modify

In each of the sentences below, underline the adverb phrase once and draw an arrow to the word or words it modifies. Several sentences contain more than one adverb phrase.

EX. 1. The geese flew over the marsh, heading south.

1. In 1348, the Black Death raged throughout Europe.
2. Once, after a big storm, we found a robin's nest.
3. Soft as a summer breeze, the music drifted across the park.
4. That building has been standing for over two thousand years.
5. The actor's agent called from New York.
6. Yolanda and her parents traveled by boat down the Amazon River.
7. Michael will arrive from Nova Scotia late in the afternoon.
8. In the United States, more than two thousand dogs are born each hour.
9. The tiny black-and-white kitten strayed far from home.
10. The jeep was parked beside a fire hydrant in a no-parking zone.

MODULE 3: THE PHRASE

VERBALS AND VERB PHRASES

Verbals are forms of verbs that are used as adjectives, nouns, or adverbs. The three kinds of verbals are *participles, gerunds*, and *infinitives*.

3e A *participle* is a verb form that can be used as an adjective.

EXAMPLES The children thought that the carnival rides were **exciting.** [*Exciting*, formed from the verb *excite*, modifies the noun *rides*.]

The **baked** potatoes tasted delicious. [*Baked*, formed from the verb *bake*, modifies the noun *potatoes*.]

(1) *Present participles* end in *–ing*.

EXAMPLES The movie was **entertaining.** [*Entertaining*, formed from the verb *entertain*, modifies the noun *movie*.]

A wild turkey wandered through the **crackling** stalks of corn. [*Crackling*, formed from the verb *crackle*, modifies the noun *stalks*.]

(2) Most *past participles* usually end in *–d* or *–ed*. A few are formed irregularly.

EXAMPLES **Dazed** and **confused,** the rider dusted himself off and climbed back onto his horse. [*Dazed* and *confused*, formed from the verbs *daze* and *confuse*, modify the noun *rider*.]

Moths and mosquitoes flew in through the **broken** window. [*Broken*, formed from the verb *break*, modifies the noun *window*.]

Both present and past participles can be used as part of a verb phrase. When used in a verb phrase, a participle is part of the verb. It is not a verbal used as an adjective.

EXAMPLES The workers **were digging** a tunnel under the river.

The window **was broken** by the hurricane's strong winds.

EXERCISE 5 Identifying Participles and the Words They Modify

Underline the participles used as adjectives in each of the following sentences. Then draw an arrow to the noun or the pronoun that each participle modifies.

EX. 1. The grass around the pond was filled with croaking frogs.

1. The graded papers are on the teacher's desk, next to her laptop.
2. A shooting star streaked across the night sky and then was gone.

3. The Sahara, a burning desert, is the hottest place on our planet.
4. The Sikh men of northern India can be recognized by their turbans, unshaven beards, and long hair.
5. Smiling broadly, Paco accepted the nomination for class president.
6. Bored, Andrea walked to the library to find a good mystery book.
7. A crow sat in a tree in the deepening twilight.
8. “This bicycle is now in good working order,” said the mechanic.
9. Satisfied, the diners paid the check and left the restaurant.
10. The telephone poles along the highway were covered with hanging vines of kudzu.
11. Peter liked wearing wrinkled suits.
12. They were looking for a reclining chair, but they bought a sofa instead.
13. The building designed by my uncle won an award.
14. Creeping thyme and roses grow all over our terrace.
15. A hand-pieced quilt is more costly than a quilt that is sewn by machine.

EXERCISE 6 Choosing Appropriate Participles

Complete the paragraph below by writing appropriate participles formed from the verbs given in parentheses. Write your answers on your own paper.

EX. [1] For English class, Malcolm wrote an (*interest*) story.
1. interesting

[1] Malcolm’s story is about a (*miss*) cat. [2] In the story, a young girl thinks that her cat has crawled through a (*tear*) window screen. [3] (*Worry*), the girl goes outside to search for her pet. [4] For several (*trouble*) hours she searches the alleyways and lawns near her house. [5] She looks everywhere for the cat—in trees, on porches, in drain pipes, and under (*park*) cars. [6] (*Discourage*), she eventually gives up the search and goes back home. [7] Back inside, she notices something (*surprise*). [8] She opens the window shades to let sunlight into her (*darken*) room and sees that the cat’s food has been eaten. [9] Then she hears a (*scratch*) sound under her bed. [10] All the time, the cat has been in a secret (*hide*) place, inside the box spring.

MODULE 3: THE PHRASE

PARTICIPIAL PHRASES

3f A *participial phrase* consists of a participle and any complements or modifiers it may have. The entire participial phrase acts as an adjective.

A participial phrase should be placed as close as possible to the word it modifies. Otherwise the sentence may not make sense.

EXAMPLES **Writing from personal experience,** Thon created a report about life in a small Vietnamese village. [The phrase *Writing from personal experience* modifies the noun *Thon.* The adjective phrase *from personal experience* modifies the participle *Writing.*]

The music **playing over the loudspeakers** was written by the composer Scott Joplin. [The phrase *playing over the loudspeakers* modifies the noun *music.* The adverb phrase *over the loudspeakers* modifies the participle *playing.*]

Completely exhausted by their climb, the hikers stopped to rest and eat some trail mix. [The phrase *Completely exhausted by their climb* modifies the noun *hikers*. The participle *exhausted* is modified by the adverb *completely* and by the adverb phrase *by their climb.*]

EXERCISE 7 Identifying Participles and Participial Phrases

In the following sentences, put brackets around the participles, and underline the participial phrases.

EX. 1. Have you seen those strange mushrooms [growing] in the cellar?

1. Working around the clock, the farmers saved the orange crop from frostbite.
2. The Somali refugees, weakened by hunger, arrived at an emergency center, where they received food and medical treatment.
3. From the plane we could see Lake Erie, shining brightly below us.
4. Nominated by President Johnson, Thurgood Marshall became the first African American Supreme Court justice.
5. The largest dinosaurs, weighing over 150 tons, were harmless plant-eaters.

6. Often costing more than gold or jewels, spices were highly prized in the Middle Ages in Europe.
7. Hidden by their markings, tigers are rarely seen in the wild.
8. Zimbabwe is an African country bordered by Zambia, Botswana, Mozambique, and South Africa.
9. Known for its hot, wet climate, Papua New Guinea produces coffee, coconuts, and cocoa.
10. Nearly destroyed by a great fire, this Midwestern city was rebuilt by its mostly immigrant population.
11. Moving forward, backward, and from side to side, the virtual reality machine gave us the exciting impression that we were floating in space.
12. My grandfather found some ancient tools lying on the floor of a cave.
13. The backpacker loved the haunting sound of wolves howling in the distance.
14. Standing skillfully on her toes, the ballerina lifted her arms toward the ceiling.
15. Reading alone in his room at night, Grant dreamed of the day when he, too, would write books that other people would read.
16. In the center of the room stood a man in a red flannel shirt, shoveling coal into the furnace.
17. We admired the stained glass windows of the cathedral.
18. Strengthened by his mother's milk, the colt grew strong and healthy.
19. Through the windows of the preschool, we could see children playing happily.
20. The directions included with the videotape player weren't in English.

MODULE 3: THE PHRASE

GERUNDS

3g A *gerund* is a verb form ending in *–ing* that is used as a noun.

Like nouns, gerunds can be subjects, predicate nominatives, direct objects, or objects of prepositions.

EXAMPLES **Skiing** is a popular winter sport. [subject]
My favorite activity is **writing.** [predicate nominative]
Marsha loves **skating.** [direct object]
Hector signed up for a class in **cooking.** [object of a preposition]

Do not confuse a gerund with a present participle used as part of a verb phrase or as an adjective.

EXAMPLES The reporters have finished **taking** pictures, but they **are** still **writing** the story. [*Taking* is a gerund used as the direct object of the verb phrase *have finished. Writing* is a present participle used as part of the verb phrase *are writing*.]

The **cleaning** crew removed the stains by **scrubbing** the carpet with brushes. [*Cleaning* is a present participle used as an adjective to modify the noun *crew. Scrubbing* is a gerund used as the object of the preposition *by*.]

EXERCISE 8 Identifying Gerunds and Their Uses

Underline the gerunds in the following sentences. Then, on the line before each sentence, identify how each gerund is used by writing *s.* for *subject, p.n.* for *predicate nominative, d.o.* for *direct object*, or *o.p.* for *object of a preposition.* Some sentences contain more than one gerund.

EX. *o.p.* 1. This is an excellent pen for drawing.

______ 1. Jogging is good exercise but should be done in moderation.

______ 2. Uncle Ned says that politicians enjoy talking.

______ 3. One popular activity of the 1980s was break dancing.

______ 4. The craft center offers classes in weaving.

______ 5. This shop sells tools and supplies for gardening.

______ 6. Sara hates cooking, but she loves eating.

______ 7. One particularly dangerous sport is rock climbing.

______ 8. Sculpting is easier when done in clay than when done in marble.

______ 9. These glasses are for reading the tiny print in the dictionary.

______ 10. A big business in the Pacific Northwest is logging.

______ 11. Ms. Horowitz studied marketing at a business school.

______ 12. Harvesting is one of the most difficult jobs on a farm.

______ 13. A writer must save time for rewriting and for editing.

______ 14. Darnelle really enjoys skating.

______ 15. Studying requires a quiet work place and a clear mind.

______ 16. How dangerous is bungee jumping?

______ 17. This wide-angle lens is for taking close-ups.

______ 18. Selling insurance may be the thing for me.

______ 19. When Lee complained about his grade, I said, "Try studying."

______ 20. I'm sorry, but I've just never enjoyed cleaning.

EXERCISE 9 Using Gerunds in Sentences

On your own paper, write a sentence for each of the following gerunds. Underline each gerund. At the end of your sentence, identify the gerund's use by writing *s.* for *subject, p.n.* for *predicate nominative, d.o.* for *direct object*, or *o.p.* for *object of a preposition*. Be sure to vary the uses of the gerunds in your sentences.

EX. 1. flying
1. *A bird needs powerful wings for flying. (o.p.)*

1. singing
2. diving
3. shopping
4. reading
5. playing
6. wrestling
7. swimming
8. waltzing
9. harmonizing
10. parking
11. dozing
12. paying
13. driving
14. listening
15. insulting
16. waiting
17. moving
18. wearing
19. dropping
20. noticing

MODULE 3: THE PHRASE

GERUND PHRASES

3h A *gerund phrase* consists of a gerund and any modifiers and complements it may have. The entire gerund phrase acts as a noun.

Like gerunds, gerund phrases can be subjects, predicate nominatives, direct objects, or objects of prepositions.

EXAMPLES **Working at the teen center** has been fun. [The phrase is the subject of the sentence. The gerund *Working* is modified by the adjective phrase *at the teen center*.]

My favorite pastime is **reading about ancient Egypt.** [The phrase is a predicate nominative. The gerund *reading* is modified by the adjective phrase *about ancient Egypt*.]

I really enjoy **learning mathematics now.** [The phrase is the direct object of the verb *enjoy*. The gerund *learning* has a direct object, *mathematics*, and is modified by the adverb *now*.]

You need special equipment for **skiing across country.** [The phrase is the object of the preposition *for*. The gerund *skiing* is modified by the adverb phrase *across country*.]

When a noun or pronoun comes immediately before a gerund, it is in the possessive form and is considered part of the gerund phrase.

EXAMPLES **Sandra's singing** woke the neighbors.
The neighbors don't really appreciate **her singing late at night.**

EXERCISE 10 Identifying Gerund Phrases and Their Uses

Underline the gerund phrases in the following sentences. On the line before each sentence, identify how each gerund phrase is used by writing *s.* for *subject, p.n.* for *predicate nominative, d.o.* for *direct object*, or *o.p.* for *object of a preposition*.

EX. *p.n.* 1. My dog's favorite activity is chewing on old shoes.

______ 1. If you see a rattlesnake in the wild, the wisest course of action is staying away from it.

______ 2. Hosting a live talk show can be quite a challenge.

______ 3. The people of Bangladesh support themselves by growing rice, tea, sugar cane, and other crops.

______ 4. The principal considered changing the school dress code.

______ 5. Washing a car can use a great deal of water.

______ 6. David Livingstone and Henry Stanley are famous for exploring the interior of Africa.

______ 7. Picasso disliked artwork that looked like photographs, so he began painting people as simple shapes, such as cubes.

______ 8. My dream has always been traveling in Latin America.

______ 9. Zebras, giraffes, wildebeests, and impala live by grazing on grasslands.

______ 10. One way politicians announce that they will run for office is by holding a press conference.

______ 11. Many people love Alice Walker's writing about life in the rural South.

______ 12. Chasing golf balls around a field isn't my idea of a good time.

______ 13. My brother Sam's hobby is building model airplanes.

______ 14. By publishing his play, *The Escape*, in 1858, William Wells Brown became the first African American playwright.

______ 15. Planning an interview takes a great deal of time and thought.

EXERCISE 11 Identifying Gerund Phrases and Their Uses

Underline the gerund phrases in the paragraph below. Then, above each gerund phrase, identify its use by writing *s.* for *subject, p.n.* for *predicate nominative, d.o.* for *direct object*, or *o.p.* for *object of a preposition.*

s.

EX. [1] Sewing fabric into useful objects is one of the practical arts.

[1] The fabric shop in our town offers classes in sewing for pleasure. [2] I've taken several classes there, but the one I liked most was "Quilting the Old-Fashioned Way." [3] Making a quilt isn't difficult to do, but it does take patience. [4] The hardest parts for me were threading needles and cutting the quilt pieces. [5] You should try making a quilt sometime. It's a great deal of fun.

MODULE 3: THE PHRASE

INFINITIVES AND INFINITIVE PHRASES

3i An *infinitive* is a verb form, usually preceded by *to,* that can be used as a noun, an adjective, or an adverb.

NOUNS Mariah loves **to dance** and **to sing.** [*To dance* and *to sing* are the direct objects of the verb *loves*.]

To read is **to escape** into another reality. [*To read* is the subject. *To escape* is a predicate nominative.]

ADJECTIVES The crossing guard is the person **to ask.** [*To ask* modifies the noun *person.*]

The ones **to thank** are your parents. [*To thank* modifies the pronoun *ones*.]

ADVERBS That horse is certain **to win.** [*To win* modifies the adjective *certain.*]
Daniel has come **to help.** [*To help* modifies the verb *has come.*]

3j An *infinitive phrase* consists of an infinitive together with its modifiers and complements. The entire infinitive phrase can be used as a noun, an adjective, or an adverb.

NOUN **To swim across the English Channel** must be very difficult. [The phrase is the subject of the sentence.]

ADJECTIVE The person **to fix your computer** is my friend, Rolf. [The phrase modifies the noun *person.*]

ADVERB Sometimes it isn't easy **to make new friends.** [The phrase modifies the adjective *easy.*]

NOTE An infinitive may have a subject.

EXAMPLE Chandra wanted **me to help her.** [*Me* is the subject of the infinitive *to help.*]

NOTE Sometimes the *to* that is the sign of the infinitive can be left out.

EXAMPLE The janitor helped us [to] **string** the lights in the auditorium.

EXERCISE 12 Identifying Infinitive Phrases and Their Function

Underline the infinitive phrases in the following sentences. Above each infinitive, identify its use by writing *s.* for *subject, p.n.* for *predicate nominative, d.o.* for *direct object, adj.* for *adjective*, or *adv.* for *adverb*.

adj.

EX. 1. The first ship to carry African Americans to the colonies arrived in Jamestown in 1619.

1. The first colony to give legal recognition to the institution of slavery was Massachusetts.
2. In another colony, New Netherlands, eleven African Americans petitioned the government to demand their freedom.
3. The first white organization to denounce slavery publicly was a group of Quakers in Germantown, Pennsylvania.
4. Crispus Attucks was killed in the Boston Massacre in 1770, becoming one of the first people to die in the troubles before the Revolutionary War.
5. To fight for freedom was one reason Americans fought and risked their lives.
6. Peter Salem and Salem Poor joined other African Americans to fight in the battles of Bunker Hill and Breed's Hill in 1775.
7. The following year, the Continental Congress approved General Washington's order to enlist free African Americans in the army.
8. In 1777, Vermont became the first American colony to abolish slavery.
9. During the Revolutionary War, African American soldiers helped to win the battles of Rhode Island, Long Island, Red Bank, Savannah, Monmouth, and Fort Griswold.
10. Rhode Island was the first colony in which enslaved people were allowed to enlist in its army.
11. To enlist in the British army and to gain their freedom were the reasons thousands of other enslaved people left their plantations.
12. In 1781, twenty-six people of African descent helped to found the city of Los Angeles, California.
13. A new law to prohibit slavery from the Northwest Territory was passed by the Continental Congress.
14. Many people were unhappy to see that the U.S. Constitution protected slavery.
15. The U.S. Congress refused to accept a legal petition from African Americans in 1797.

MODULE 3: THE PHRASE

REVIEW EXERCISE

A. Identifying and Classifying Prepositional Phrases

Underline the prepositional phrases in the sentences below. Above each phrase, write *adj. phr.* for *adjective phrase* or *adv. phr.* for *adverb phrase*.

adv. phr.

EX. 1. Hervé showed us how to use a level.

1. The meeting of the prom committee lasted late into the evening.
2. A bat flew through the window and landed on the sofa.
3. A house with seven windows stands near the old courthouse.
4. A platypus looks like a prehistoric animal.
5. The antenna on the roof swayed in the wind.
6. The Maoris of New Zealand were fierce warriors who fought with clubs of bone or stone.
7. Singapore is a small country in Southeast Asia.
8. The people with the most packages helped first.
9. The Burj Khalifa in the United Arab Emirates and the Shanghai Tower in China are two of the tallest buildings in the world.
10. The capital of West Virginia is Charleston, and the capital of Virginia is Richmond.

B. Identifying Verbals and Verbal Phrases

Underline the verbals and verbal phrases in the following sentences. Then, on the line before each sentence, identify each by writing *part.* for *participle, part. phr.* for *participial phrase, ger.* for *gerund, ger. phr.* for *gerund phrase, inf.* for *infinitive*, or *inf. phr.* for *infinitive phrase*.

EX. *inf. phr.* 1. Carole loves to collect beach glass by the ocean.

__________ 1. Fencing is a popular sport and is an event in the Olympic Games.

__________ 2. The writer was asked to create a screenplay from a contemporary novel.

__________ 3. The clouds looked like a caravan of camels moving across the sky.

______ 4. Laughing at your troubles can make you feel happier.

______ 5. To build a fire in a rainstorm, you need shelter and some waterproof matches.

______ 6. Soledad wants to act, so she studies at night at the school of dramatic arts.

______ 7. Smiling, the clown handed the child a bright red balloon.

______ 8. Marc likes playing the infield, but I prefer the outfield.

______ 9. One of the most unusual of all occupations is operating a dirigible.

______ 10. Collecting specimens in the Amazon rain forest, the scientist discovered several previously unknown species.

______ 11. The computer sitting on the table is a color laptop.

______ 12. Nathan actually enjoys doing the dishes.

______ 13. Turtles return to land to lay their eggs.

______ 14. Flowing through a low plain in Ireland, the Shannon is the longest river in all of the British Isles.

______ 15. The polar bear, captured by park rangers, was released in the wild, far from any towns or cities.

______ 16. One of the most useful and ancient of all the arts is weaving.

______ 17. Emilio says that Chicago is a nice place to live.

______ 18. On our hike we saw an owl sitting quietly on the branches of a spruce.

______ 19. To build Stonehenge, prehistoric people cut and moved stones that weighed about thirty tons.

______ 20. In the 1800s and in the early 1900s, women campaigned for the right to vote.

C. Writing a Fax with Verbals and Verbal Phrases

You are part of a research team living underwater in a specially built vessel. You can send a fax to the upper world once a month. However, your fax is limited to ten sentences. On your own paper, write a fax to a friend, telling him or her what you've been doing or what you've seen. In your fax, use at least one participle or participial phrase, one gerund or gerund phrase, and one infinitive or infinitive phrase. Underline each verbal or verbal phrase and label it *part.* for *participle, part. phr.* for *participial phrase, ger.* for *gerund, ger. phr.* for *gerund phrase, inf.* for *infinitive*, or *inf. phr.* for *infinitive phrase.*

EX. *We've been trying to grow plants (inf. phr.) in our controlled atmosphere.*

MODULE 3: THE PHRASE

APPOSITIVES AND APPOSITIVE PHRASES

3k An *appositive* is a noun or pronoun placed beside another noun or pronoun to identify or explain it.

EXAMPLES Chris Johnson, the **president,** spoke to the graduating class. [The noun *president* is an appositive that identifies the noun *Chris Johnson.*] We gave it to him, a **writer,** for revising. [The noun *writer* is an appositive that identifies the pronoun *him.*]

3l An *appositive phrase* is made up of an appositive and its modifiers.

EXAMPLES The slide show was presented by Ms. Vasquez, **the director of the museum.**

The painting, **a work in the style of Mary Cassatt,** hangs in my grandmother's living room.

An appositive phrase usually follows the noun or pronoun it refers to. Sometimes, though, it comes before the noun or pronoun.

EXAMPLE **Atalented magician,** Marc pretended to break an egg and then put it back together again.

NOTE Appositives and appositive phrases are often set off by commas. Use commas if the appositive or appositive phrase is not needed to identify uniquely the noun or pronoun to which it refers.

EXAMPLES My brother, **Nathaniel,** is a sculptor. [The writer has only one brother. Therefore, the appositive, *Nathaniel,* is not needed in order to identify the brother.]

My brother **Nathaniel** is a sculptor. [The writer has more than one brother. Therefore, the appositive is needed in order to identify the brother.]

EXERCISE 13 Identifying Appositives and Appositive Phrases

Underline the appositives and appositive phrases in the following sentences.

EX. 1. The winners of the soccer match, the Fifth Street Spikers, celebrated at a local restaurant.

1. My oldest sister, Susan, is a lawyer in New York City.
2. Sequoyah, a Cherokee, invented an alphabet for the Cherokee language.
3. I read Sheila's poem, a ballad, over the public-address system at school.

4. Hector says that he prefers to write in Spanish, his first language.
5. My friend Miguel wants to travel to Australia and New Zealand.
6. We swam in the pool belonging to our neighbors, the Sironises.
7. Denise's father, a tireless worker, volunteers at a shelter for homeless women and children.
8. Across our lawn and into the woods, the fox, a bright orange creature, ran.
9. This brand of cereal, a new product, contains no sugar or fat.
10. In high school, Pilar founded a student newspaper, *The Hamilton High Herald.*
11. This plant, a kind of fern, grows along riverbanks.
12. Have you seen Toshiro's new electric guitar, the one with the sunburst design?
13. Edie, an old friend of mine, now lives in Pennsylvania.
14. In history class we are studying the reign of the Roman emperor Julius Caesar.
15. Beeswax, a material used in candles, can be purchased at a hobby or crafts shop.
16. The storm, a hurricane, spent itself off the coast and caused little damage.
17. Jake is interested in the history of the Hopi, a people of the American Southwest.
18. Outside the United States, cookstoves for camping often require kerosene, a kind of thin oil.
19. Have you written a thank-you note to your cousin Margaret?
20. The car, an antique, was on display in the middle of the shopping mall.

MODULE 3: THE PHRASE

MODULE REVIEW

A. Identifying and Classifying Prepositional Phrases

Underline the prepositional phrases in the sentences below. Above each phrase, write *adj. phr.* for *adjective phrase* or *adv. phr.* for *adverb phrase.* Some sentences contain more than one phrase.

EX. 1. The anxious dancer waited in the wings. (*adv. phr.*)

1. The start of the game was delayed by rain.
2. Waste water flows directly into the river.
3. A museum guide showed us some photographs from the 1930s.
4. All the walnuts and chestnuts have fallen from the trees.
5. I spent the morning at my uncle's house.
6. Tina works with small children in a day care center.
7. Mr. Sanchez planted beautiful sunflowers along the back fence.
8. Do you know the nursery rhyme about Mary and the little lamb?
9. Near the park is a small bakery owned by Mr. and Ms. Paulsen.
10. Have you seen the ring around the moon?
11. Some houses are heated with solar energy.
12. Madeleine lived in an old house in Paris.
13. Mr. Johnson slept through the second act.
14. The horse rose on its hind legs and pawed at the sky.
15. Did you attend the powwow in Albuquerque?

B. Identifying Verbal Phrases and Appositive Phrases

Underline the verbal and appositive phrases in the following sentences. Then, on the line before each sentence, identify each by writing *part. phr.* for *participial phrase, ger. phr.* for *gerund phrase, inf. phr.* for *infinitive phrase*, or *app. phr.* for *appositive phrase*.

EX. *app. phr.* 1. The grizzly, a mother with two cubs, chased some campers away.

__________ 1. My fantasy is writing the perfect one-act play.

__________ 2. To master these techniques, you must have patience.

__________ 3. Waving to the crowd, the queen stepped into the airplane.

__________ 4. Working the early morning shift can be exhausting.

__________ 5. The bird, a bright red cardinal, stood out against the white snow and the black branches of the trees.

__________ 6. The rabbi's message was that we must learn to love others and ourselves.

__________ 7. Did you see those kids coasting down the hill?

__________ 8. Arturo, the new student from Argentina, told us about the gauchos.

__________ 9. Marike likes studying early in the morning.

__________ 10. Totally surprised by the president's announcement, the Congress went into an emergency session.

__________ 11. The maple tree in the back yard grew to be quite tall.

__________ 12. Rolling in from the ocean, a thick fog covered the whole city.

__________ 13. Is Kerry a good driver because she has mastered parallel parking?

__________ 14. Mr. McGregor found a diamond ring lying on the sidewalk.

__________ 15. Going down the rabbit hole led Alice into many strange adventures.

C. Writing Sentences with Phrases

Write ten sentences, following the directions below. Underline the italicized phrase in each of your sentences.

EX. 1. Use *along the highway* as an adjective phrase.
1. *Have you noticed all the new billboards along the highway?*

1. Use *of the house* as an adjective phrase.
2. Use *as a feather* as an adverb phrase.
3. Use *in the hallway* as an adjective phrase.
4. Use *by airplane* as an adverb phrase.
5. Use *lighting his way with a torch* as a participial phrase.
6. Use *learning lines for a play* as a gerund phrase that is the subject of the sentence.
7. Use the infinitive phrase *to study Chinese* as the direct object of the verb.
8. Use the infinitive phrase *to visit Thailand with her parents* as an adverb phrase.
9. Use *a kind of reference work* as an appositive phrase.
10. Use *my youngest sister* as an appositive phrase.

MODULE 4: THE CLAUSE

KINDS OF CLAUSES

A ***clause*** is a group of words that contains a verb and its subject. There are two kinds of clauses, *independent* and *subordinate.*

4a An *independent* (or *main*) *clause* expresses a complete thought and can stand alone as a sentence.

S V

EXAMPLES **Roberto Clemente was a great baseball player.** [This entire sentence is an independent clause.]

S V S V

His lifetime batting average was .317 and **he had 3,000 hits.** [This sentence contains two independent clauses.]

S V S V

Clemente was born in Puerto Rico in 1934; in 1972, he was killed in a plane crash. [This sentence contains two independent clauses.]

S V

Clemente helped the Pittsburgh Pirates win the World Series

S V

in 1971; he got a hit in every single World Series game. [This sentence contains two independent clauses.]

4b A *subordinate* (or *dependent*) *clause* does not express a complete thought and cannot stand alone as a sentence.

Subordinate means "less important." A word such as *who, that, because, if, when, although,* or *since* signals that the clause it introduces is subordinate. The subordinate clause must be joined to an independent clause to make a complete sentence.

SUBORDINATE CLAUSES because I won the election

that I read aloud in class

who loaned me a pen

SENTENCES **Because I won the election,** I am now the class president.

The poem **that I read aloud in class** is by Maya Angelou.

I don't know the student **who loaned me a pen.**

As these example sentences show, a subordinate clause may appear at the beginning, the middle, or the end of a sentence.

EXERCISE 1 Identifying Independent and Subordinate Clauses

Identify the italicized clauses in the paragraph below by writing *indep.* for *independent* or *sub.* for *subordinate* on the line before each sentence.

EX. [1] sub. *When she died in 1993 at the age of ninety-seven,* Dr. Stella Kramrisch was a world-famous expert on the art and culture of India.

[1] _______________ *Stella Kramrisch was born on May 29, 1896, in Mikulov, Moravia.* [2] _______________ *When she was a young girl,* she and her parents moved to Vienna, Austria. [3] _______________ *When she was a young student,* she discovered her interest in the art and literature of India, something she pursued all her life. [4] _______________ *She enrolled at the University of Vienna,* where she studied Indian art and philosophy, Sanskrit, and anthropology. [5] _______________ *After she earned her doctorate in 1919,* Dr. Kramrisch traveled to England to give a lecture at Oxford University. [6] _______________ Rabindranath Tagore, *who was a great Indian poet,* attended her lecture. [7] _______________ He invited Dr. Kramrisch to return to India with him and teach at a university *that he had founded.* [8] _______________ She taught in India for almost thirty years; *then she traveled to the United States and became a professor at the University of Pennsylvania.* [9] _______________ *While she taught,* she also wrote many books on Indian art and culture. [10] _______________ She became the curator of the Philadelphia Museum of Art in 1954. *Today, thanks to Dr. Stella Kramrisch, the museum has one of the most important collections of Indian art.* [11] _______________ *Dr. Kramrisch worked at the museum until 1972,* when she retired. [12] _______________ *Although she was in her seventies,* she continued to help the museum for nearly twenty more years. [13] _______________ *She wrote many important books, including her masterwork, The Hindu Temple.* [14] _______________ When she died, *she was at her home.* [15] _______________ She will be honored and missed by the museum *because of her great contributions.*

MODULE 4: THE CLAUSE

THE ADJECTIVE CLAUSE

4c An *adjective clause* is a subordinate clause that modifies a noun or a pronoun.

An adjective clause always directly follows the word it modifies. If the clause is necessary, or *essential*, to the meaning of the sentence, it is not set off by commas. If the clause simply adds information and is *nonessential* to the meaning of the sentence, commas are used to set it off.

EXAMPLES Men **who are competing in the cooking contest** should know how to make chili. [The clause is necessary to identify *which men*; therefore, it is not set off by commas.]

The cooking contest, **which is open to both male and female cooks,** will be held in the convention hall. [The clause adds nonessential information; therefore, it is set off by commas.]

An adjective clause is usually introduced by a ***relative pronoun*** which ***relates*** the clause to the word that the clause modifies.

Relative Pronouns				
who	whom	whose	which	that

EXAMPLES I have an uncle **who is a teacher at Tuskegee University.** [The relative pronoun *who* relates the adjective clause to the noun *uncle*.]

Tuskegee University, **which is in Alabama,** was founded by Booker T. Washington. [The relative pronoun *which* relates the adjective clause to the proper noun *Tuskegee University*.]

Sometimes the relative pronoun may be left out of a sentence. In such cases, the relative pronoun is understood, but it still has a function in the adjective clause.

EXAMPLE Biology is the course **[that] my uncle teaches.** [The understood relative pronoun *that* relates the adjective clause to the noun *course*.]

The relative adverbs *where* and *when* are sometimes used to introduce adjective clauses.

EXAMPLES Here is the classroom **where my uncle teaches biology.**
This is the time **when he holds conferences**.

EXERCISE 2 Identifying Adjective Clauses

In each sentence below, underline the adjective clause once and the relative pronoun or relative adverb twice. Then, on the line before the sentence, write the noun or pronoun that the adjective clause modifies.

EX. *artist* 1. Leonardo da Vinci was the artist who painted the *Mona Lisa*.

_________ 1. Most people today refer to him as "Leonardo," which was his first name.

_________ 2. Besides his famous paintings, Leonardo made many scientific drawings that were ahead of his time.

_________ 3. He drew plans for a flying machine that is very similar to a modern helicopter.

_________ 4. Leonardo lived in a time when such machines could not be made.

_________ 5. Leonardo was born in 1452 near Vinci, which is a village in central Italy.

_________ 6. He studied painting with a well-known painter whose name was Andrea del Verrocchio.

_________ 7. The painting that made Leonardo most famous is known as the *Mona Lisa*.

_________ 8. The painting shows a woman who has a gentle, mysterious smile.

_________ 9. Francis I, who was the king of France, bought the painting from Leonardo.

_________ 10. Today, the Louvre in Paris is the place where people may see it.

MODULE 4: THE CLAUSE

THE ADVERB CLAUSE

4d An *adverb clause* is a subordinate clause that modifies a verb, an adjective, or an adverb.

An adverb clause tells *how, where, when, why, to what extent*, or *under what conditions*.

EXAMPLES **Because it was raining,** we came inside. [The adverb clause tells *why* we came inside. It modifies the verb *came*.]

Georgia is taller **than I am.** [The adverb clause tells *to what extent* Georgia is tall. It modifies the adjective *taller*.]

If we hurry, we can catch that bus. [The adverb clause tells *under what conditions* we can catch the bus. It modifies the verb phrase *can catch*.]

NOTE As the first and third examples above show, an adverb clause at the beginning of a sentence is usually set off by a comma.

An adverb clause is introduced by a ***subordinating conjunction***, a word that relates the adverb clause to the word or words that the clause modifies.

Common Subordinating Conjunctions			
after	as though	since	when
although	because	so that	whenever
as	before	than	where
as if	even though	though	wherever
as long as	if	unless	whether
as soon as	in order that	until	while

Some subordinating conjunctions, such as *after, as, before, since*, and *until*, can also be prepositions.

SUBORDINATING CONJUNCTION **After we ate lunch,** we went to the museum.

PREPOSITION **After lunch,** we went to the museum.

EXERCISE 3 Identifying Adverb Clauses and Subordinating Conjunctions

In each sentence below, underline the adverb clause once and the subordinating conjunction twice.

EX. 1. Whenever we climb Mount Katahdin, we are thrilled by the view.

1. I was late this morning because I forgot to set my alarm clock.
2. Please call my uncle Raphael when you arrive in San Juan.
3. As soon as the towels are dry, please fold them and put them away.
4. The hill was steeper than we had expected.
5. Why did the doctor act as if she were worried?
6. He wears a hairpiece, though you wouldn't have guessed.
7. Before I eat dinner, may I have a cup of tea?
8. If you don't clean your room, you'll be grounded.
9. We were worried until we got the message from Chen.
10. I need to know whether your mom can drive us to the concert.

EXERCISE 4 Building Sentences That Have Adverb Clauses

On your own paper, write five sentences. To create your sentences, choose two clauses from the list below. Combine these clauses with subordinating conjunctions from the chart in section 5d. Do not use any subordinating conjunction twice. Underline the adverb clauses in your sentences once and the subordinating conjunctions twice.

EX. 1. she caught the ball the sun was in her eyes

1. *Although the sun was in her eyes, she caught the ball.*

Eleni wrote to me
someone phoned Barbara
we went to the concert
it was raining
she was on vacation
we had to reschedule the meeting
she was in Mexico
we needed a ride home
I had a cold
Jeremy arrived late

we missed the bus
they made the decorations
you helped
we played a game of checkers
they arrived
we ordered our dinner
Delores came to the party
she read my poem aloud
he told a funny joke
I felt unhappy

MODULE 4: THE CLAUSE

THE NOUN CLAUSE

4e A *noun clause* is a subordinate clause used as a noun.

A noun clause may be used as a subject, a predicate nominative, a direct object, an indirect object, or the object of a preposition.

SUBJECT	**Whoever wins the race** will claim the trophy.
PREDICATE NOMINATIVE	His wish is **that he will become a famous singer**.
DIRECT OBJECT	I hope **that you will come to my party**.
INDIRECT OBJECT	He will give **whomever he chooses** the extra ticket.
OBJECT OF A PREPOSITION	We are proud of **what we have accomplished**.

As these examples show, a noun clause is usually introduced by a word such as *that, what, when, where, whether, who, whoever, whom, whomever, whose*, or *why*. Sometimes, however, the word that introduces a noun clause may be omitted.

EXAMPLE She told me **you won the election**. [The introductory word *that* is understood. The noun clause is the direct object of the verb *told*.]

EXERCISE 5 Identifying and Classifying Noun Clauses

Underline the noun clause in each of the following sentences. Then, on the line before the sentence, tell how the noun clause is used in the sentence. Write *s.* for *subject, p.n.* for *predicate nominative, d.o.* for *direct object, i.o.* for *indirect object*, or *o.p.* for *object of a preposition.*

EX. *o.p.* 1. Waneta has promised a reward to whoever finds her cat.

_______ 1. What we need is an after-school recreation program.

_______ 2. Dr. Donato said that she could meet with us next Tuesday.

_______ 3. That Rita Moreno is a talented actress has been proven by her many great performances.

_______ 4. Would you please give whoever wants one, a ticket to the game?

_______ 5. The art teacher always takes great interest in what we create.

_______ 6. The coach will make whoever scores the most points the "Athlete of the Week."

_______ 7. How you can memorize poems so quickly really amazes me.

_______ 8. My dentist told me I may need a filling.

_______ 9. Will you tell me who sent these roses?

_____ 10. Many people in the group believed that we should serve fried plantains at the dinner.

EXERCISE 6 Creating Sentences by Inserting Noun Clauses

On your own paper, create sentences by inserting noun clauses in the blanks provided. Use the introductory word shown in parentheses.

EX. 1. Eliza told me _______________. (Use *that.*)

1. *Eliza told me that Ramon is going to the carnival tonight.*

1. I will loan the money to _______________. (Use *whoever.*)
2. _______________ is obvious. (Use *that.*)
3. The best part of the show was _______________. (Use *when.*)
4. _______________ will be right. (Use *whatever.*)
5. John told me _______________. (Use *that.*)
6. The teacher will give _______________ a free pass to the game. (Use *whoever.*)
7. Did he tell you _______________? (Use *whether.*)
8. Do you know _______________? (Use *what.*)
9. The question was, _______________? (Use *Where.*)
10. _______________ is a good question. (Use *whom.*)
11. Martina believes _______________. (Use *that.*)
12. _______________ is a secret. (Use *who.*)
13. _______________ will love it. (Use *whomever.*)
14. I don't know _______________. (Use *whose.*)
15. She told me _______________. (Use *why.*)

MODULE 4: THE CLAUSE

SENTENCE STRUCTURE

The *structure* of a sentence is determined by the number and types of clauses it has.

4f According to their structure, sentences are classified as *simple, compound, complex*, or *compound-complex*.

(1) A *simple sentence* has one independent clause and no subordinate clauses. It may have a compound subject, a compound predicate, and any number of phrases.

EXAMPLES

S S V
Kiki and **Toni came** to my house for dinner last night.

S V V
After dinner, the **three** of us **compared** our notes and **outlined** our report.

(2) A *compound sentence* has two or more independent clauses and no subordinate clauses.

A compound sentence is actually two or more simple sentences joined by a comma and a coordinating conjunction, by a semicolon, or by a semicolon and a conjunctive adverb such as *therefore, however*, or *consequently*.

EXAMPLES

S V S
Kiki will write the first draft of the report, and **Toni will revise** it.

S V S S V
Kiki had some great ideas; **Toni** and **I listened** carefully.

S V S V
Toni is the best artist in the group; therefore, **she will illustrate** the report.

(3) A *complex sentence* has one independent clause and at least one subordinate clause.

EXAMPLE

S V S V
After **we discussed** our plans, **I felt** eager to begin writing.

(4) A *compound-complex sentence* has two or more independent clauses and at least one subordinate clause.

EXAMPLE

S V S V
Because the **report is** due next Tuesday, **we will work** all

S V
weekend, and **Toni will finish** her illustrations by Monday.

EXERCISE 7 Classifying Sentences According to Structure

Classify the sentences in the following paragraph. On the line before each sentence, write *simp.* for *simple, comp.* for *compound, cx.* for *complex*, or *cd.-cx.* for *compound-complex*.

EX. [1] ___*cx.*___ Although he isn't a sumo wrestler himself, Yoshiro Namekata is famous because of the sport.

[1] _______________ The sumo wrestlers of Japan wear their hair in special topknots. [2] _______________ Because the topknots are difficult to make, the wrestlers must go to expert hairdressers. [3] _______________ Yoshiro Namekata is a man who has become one of the sumo wrestlers' most popular hairstylists. [4] _______________ As a young man, Namekata didn't plan on a career as a hairdresser; in fact, he wanted to be a sumo wrestler. [5] _______________ However, sumo wrestlers must be very large and strong, and Namekata did not grow as large as he needed to be. [6] _______________ Nevertheless, with his sumo hairstyling skills, he plays an important role in Japan's traditional sport. [7] _______________ There are two basic hairstyles for sumo wrestlers, and Namekata must be an expert at both of them. [8] _______________ Top-level wrestlers get their hair styled in a domed knot, which is called an *oicho-mage*, but lower-level wrestlers get a simpler, flatter knot, the *chonmage*. [9] _______________ Most knots take Namekata at least thirty minutes to create. [10] _______________ He is a very busy man; when they are competing, Japan's top sumo wrestlers ask Namekata to style their hair twice a day.

MODULE 4: THE CLAUSE

MODULE REVIEW

A. Identifying Independent and Subordinate Clauses

In the sentences below, identify the italicized clauses. On the line before each sentence, write *indep.* if the clause is independent and *sub.* if the clause is subordinate.

EX. ___*sub.*___ 1. Edna St. Vincent Millay, *who was an American poet*, wrote many beautiful sonnets.

__________ 1. Pierre's uncle Lucien lives in the city of Chartres, *which is an hour's drive from Paris*.

__________ 2. *How hard you study* will affect your test score.

__________ 3. Simone painted a picture of the apple orchard, but *I have misplaced the picture*.

__________ 4. *When he reached his final years*, Leonardo da Vinci lived near the small French village of Amboise; modern visitors can see his house there.

__________ 5. The company *that rebuilt many of Philadelphia's historic row houses* is owned by my neighbor.

__________ 6. He told me *his grandmother came to the United States in 1975*.

__________ 7. The committee will remain *until they reach a decision*.

__________ 8. Julio has repaired many cars; in fact, *he has become extremely successful as a race car mechanic*.

__________ 9. *Gloria Ramírez sent me this postcard* while she was visiting her grandmother in Mexico.

__________ 10. I will call you *as soon as I get home from football practice*.

B. Classifying Clauses in Sentences

Classify the italicized clauses in the following paragraph. On the line before each sentence, write *adj.* for *adjective clause, adv.* for *adverb clause*, or *n.* for *noun clause*. Some sentences contain more than one clause.

EX. [1] ___*adj.*___ Clementine Hunter, *who was an African American folk artist*, was about 101 years old when she died in 1988.

[1] _____________ Clementine Hunter's paintings show *what her life was like.*

[2] _____________ In the 1940s, *when she was middle aged,* she began painting pictures about life at Melrose Plantation in northern Louisiana. [3] _____________ *While she was a house servant at the plantation*, she also worked in the fields.

[4] _____________ Over the next forty-five years, she created several thousand paintings *that use bright, clear colors*. [5] _____________ *Whatever surfaces she used for her paintings*, including canvas, cardboard, and paper, did not affect her style.

[6] _____________ With vivid colors, she painted scenes *that show the many activities of the farm workers at Melrose.* [7] _____________ There are pictures of workers *who are tending animals or gardens*, and there are others *that show the workers at dances and picnics*. [8] _____________ The African American Museum, *which is located in Dallas, Texas*, has organized a show of almost one hundred of Clementine Hunter's paintings. [9] _____________ *That Hunter was a talented painter and storyteller* is clearly seen in the many different paintings in the collection. [10] _____________ *The great popularity of the traveling exhibit* is what artists everywhere dream of achieving.

C. Writing Sentences with Varied Structures

Follow each set of directions to create your own sentences. Write your sentences on your own paper.

EX. 1. a complex sentence with a noun clause used as the subject

1. *What I need is a new notebook.*

1. a simple sentence with a compound subject
2. a simple sentence with a compound verb
3. a compound sentence with two independent clauses joined by the conjunction *and*
4. a compound sentence with two independent clauses joined by a semicolon
5. a compound sentence with two independent clauses joined by a semicolon and the conjunctive adverb *therefore*

MODULE 5: AGREEMENT

NUMBER

Number is the form of a word that indicates whether the word is singular or plural.

5a When a word refers to one person or thing, it is *singular* in number. When a word refers to more than one, it is *plural* in number.

Singular	stereo	woman	he	wolf	myself
Plural	stereos	women	they	wolves	ourselves

In general, nouns ending in –*s* are plural (*shirts, reports, horses, valleys*); verbs ending in –*s* are singular (*brings, makes, goes, has, is*).

EXERCISE 1 Identifying Words as Singular or Plural in Number

On the line before each of the following words, write *sing.* for *singular* or *pl.* for *plural*.

EX. *pl.* 1. mice

_______ 1. I
_______ 2. country
_______ 3. them
_______ 4. goes
_______ 5. she
_______ 6. children
_______ 7. crews
_______ 8. two
_______ 9. himself
_______ 10. programmer
_______ 11. yourselves
_______ 12. knives
_______ 13. laughs
_______ 14. geese
_______ 15. were
_______ 16. newspaper
_______ 17. men
_______ 18. dishes
_______ 19. tastes
_______ 20. us
_______ 21. people
_______ 22. night
_______ 23. intermission
_______ 24. handrails

_______ 25. prizes

_______ 26. breakfast

_______ 27. winners

_______ 28. thunderstorms

_______ 29. month

_______ 30. tides

_______ 31. developments

_______ 32. history

_______ 33. cities

_______ 34. airplane

_______ 35. conversation

_______ 36. planets

_______ 37. mice

_______ 38. she

_______ 39. recipe

_______ 40. feet

_______ 41. summer

_______ 42. myself

_______ 43. holds

_______ 44. grapefruits

_______ 45. waterfront

_______ 46. tugboat

_______ 47. detailers

_______ 48. follows

_______ 49. their

_______ 50. excitement

EXERCISE 2 Using Singular Subjects and Plural Subjects in Sentences

Rewrite each sentence below on your own paper. Change the singular subjects to plural and the plural subjects to singular. Be sure to make each verb agree with its subject.

EX. 1. The dog barks.
1. *The dogs bark.*

1. The actor dances.
2. Lloyd's brother cooks dinner.
3. Is the door closed?
4. The chickens supply us with eggs.
5. The vegetable gardens are planted.
6. The barn belongs to his family.
7. The turquoise stone is beautiful to see.
8. Victor's friends wait for him.
9. The mountain bikes are two-wheeled vehicles.
10. Does the meeting start tomorrow?

MODULE 5: AGREEMENT

SUBJECT-VERB AGREEMENT

5b A verb should agree with its subject in number.

(1) Singular subjects take singular verbs.

EXAMPLE The peach **seems** ripe. [The singular verb *seems* agrees with the singular subject *peach.*]

(2) Plural subjects take plural verbs.

EXAMPLE The peaches **seem** ripe. [The plural verb *seem* agrees with the plural subject *peaches*.]

Verb phrases also agree in number with their subjects. In a verb phrase, only the first auxiliary (helping) verb changes form to agree with the subject.

SINGULAR The swimmer **is diving** into the pool.
PLURAL The swimmers **are diving** into the pool.
SINGULAR **Has** the swimmer **started** the race?
PLURAL **Have** the swimmers **started** the race?

The form *were* is plural except when used with the singular *you* and in sentences that are contrary to fact.

EXAMPLES **You were** the best player on the team. [*You* is the singular subject.]
If he were captain, we would be a stronger team. [The statement is contrary to fact, for he is not the captain.]

EXERCISE 3 Selecting Verbs That Agree in Number with Their Subjects

For each of the following phrases, underline the verb or verb phrase in parentheses that agrees in number with the subject given.

EX. 1. they (*needs, <u>need</u>*)

1. Joan (*says, say*)
2. apartment (*seems, seem*)
3. bread (*tastes, taste*)
4. men (*hopes, hope*)
5. cat (*jumps, jump*)
6. we (*wishes, wish*)
7. children (*plays, play*)
8. horse (*eats, eat*)
9. dishes (*breaks, break*)
10. class (*has started, have started*)

11. you (was, were)
12. geese (is flying, are flying)
13. wax (has dried, have dried)
14. we (is riding, are riding)
15. boxes (is packed, are packed)
16. team members (was voting, were voting)
17. benches (has been built, have been built)
18. George (has finished, have finished)
19. he (has been sleeping, have been sleeping)
20. mice (has been nibbling, have been nibbling)

EXERCISE 4 Identifying Verbs That Agree in Number with Their Subjects

For each sentence below, underline the verb or verb phrase in parentheses that agrees in number with the subject.

EX. 1. The houses (*needs,* <u>*need*</u>) new roofs.

1. Laura Pausini (*is, are*) a popular singer.
2. The car (*has, have*) a flat tire.
3. Ella Mae and Julio (*is playing, are playing*) the piano.
4. She (*enjoys, enjoy*) fast-pitch softball.
5. (*Was, Were*) Willie Mays a fantastic baseball player?
6. They (*has begun, have begun*) a new project.
7. You (*was asking, were asking*) interesting questions.
8. The children (*was skating, were skating*) at the rink.
9. If I (*was, were*) president, I'd reorganize the club.
10. Somebody (*has borrowed, have borrowed*) my tennis racket.
11. (*Has, Have*) you ever heard of the tennis player Roger Federer?
12. While Donald (*is reading, are reading*), we should listen.
13. Because she (*was, were*) my best friend, I helped her.
14. The Taj Mahal (*stands, stand*) like a jewel in the sun.
15. (*Do, Does*) morning walks make you feel better?

MODULE 5: AGREEMENT

INTERVENING PHRASES

5c The number of the subject is not changed by a phrase following the subject.

The subject of a sentence is never part of a prepositional phrase.

EXAMPLES The **man** with the dark glasses **is** a famous singer. [*man is*]
The **women** on that team **are** great players. [*women are*]

Prepositional phrases may begin with compound prepositions such as *together with, in addition to, as well as*, and *along with*. These phrases do not affect the number of the verb. A verb agrees in number with its subject.

EXAMPLES **Rafael,** as well as Jim and Tony, **is** a fantastic soccer player. [*Rafael is*]
My **suitcases,** along with my duffel bag, **were** loaded onto the plane. [*suitcases were*]

A negative construction following the subject does not change the number of the subject.

EXAMPLES **Ellen,** not Peter and Julio, **has made** the posters. [*Ellen has made*]
The **chickens,** not his prize ram, **have won** the blue ribbon. [*chickens have won*]

EXERCISE 5 Identifying Verbs That Agree in Number with Their Subjects

For each of the following sentences, underline the verb or verb phrase in parentheses that agrees in number with the subject.

EX. 1. A bag of groceries (<u>*has fallen*</u>, *have fallen*) off the kitchen counter.

1. The girls on the tennis team (*is playing, are playing*) in a tournament.
2. Members of the music club (*is having, are having*) a concert tonight.
3. My dog, as well as my two cats, (*needs, need*) a rabies shot every year.
4. For me, the best poems in the entire book (*was written, were written*) by Maya Angelou.
5. The new exhibit by the Puerto Rican artists (*has been, have been*) well attended.
6. Those comedians we saw last week at that theater in the city (*was, were*) really funny.
7. The platter, along with the plates and glasses, (*was, were*) clean.

8. The horses, not the sheep or the cow, (*has been fed, have been fed*).
9. Thunder, as well as lightning and dark clouds, (*means, mean*) a storm is gathering.
10. Vivian, not her sisters, (*is, are*) making Uncle Remo's birthday cake.

EXERCISE 6 Proofreading a Paragraph for Correct Subject-Verb Agreement

In the paragraph below, draw a line through each verb or verb phrase that does not agree with its subject. Write the correct form of the verb or verb phrase in the space above the incorrect word or phrase. Some sentences may contain no agreement errors.

teaches
EX. [1] Elizabeth Yastrzemski, not her cousins, ~~teach~~ in-line skating.

[1] A family of athletes live in Long Island, New York. [2] The name of the family is Yastrzemski. [3] One of the most famous of this large group of cousins are Carl Yastrzemski. [4] Carl, for many years, were a great baseball player and a member of the Boston Red Sox. [5] Each of the other cousins enjoy sports, too. [6] The youngest cousin of the group are Elizabeth Yastrzemski. [7] She, unlike her older cousins, have chosen in-line skating as her sport. [8] Use of helmets and pads on the knees, wrists, and elbows are important in this sport, as Elizabeth knows well. [9] In-line skating, together with roller-skating and street hockey, are sports accomplished on cement. [10] This kind of skating, like many other sports, require practice.

MODULE 5: AGREEMENT

AGREEMENT WITH INDEFINITE PRONOUNS

An ***indefinite pronoun*** is a pronoun that refers to a person, place, or thing not specifically named. When used as the subject of a sentence, an indefinite pronoun must agree with its verb in number.

5d A singular indefinite pronoun must take a singular verb. The following indefinite pronouns are singular: *each, either, neither, one, everyone, everybody, no one, nobody, anyone, anybody, someone*, and *somebody*.

Notice that a phrase or a clause following one of these pronouns does not affect the number of the verb.

EXAMPLES **Everybody** on this project **is** working hard.
Neither of them **has** finished.
Someone who wears glasses **has** left them on the bus.

5e A plural indefinite pronoun must take a plural verb. The following indefinite pronouns are plural: *several, few, both*, and *many*.

EXAMPLES **Many** of my friends **have** seen that movie.
A **few** in the room **have** finished the test.

5f The indefinite pronouns *some, all, any, most*, and *none* may be either singular or plural, depending on the words they refer to.

These pronouns are singular when they refer to a singular word and plural when they refer to a plural word.

SINGULAR **Most** of the milk **has** been drunk. [*Most* refers to *milk.*]
PLURAL **Most** of the women **have** arrived. [*Most* refers to *women.*]
SINGULAR **None** of the wood **is** wet. [*None* refers to *wood.*]
PLURAL **None** of the bicycles **have** been sold. [*None* refers to *bicycles*.]

EXERCISE 7 Writing Sentences with Verbs That Agree with Their Subjects

On the lines provided, rewrite each of the following sentences. Follow the directions that appear in parentheses. If necessary, change the number of the verb to agree with the subject.

EX. 1. Everyone on the team plays well. (Change *everyone* to *all of the players*.)

All of the players on the team play well.

1. No one in my class knows the answer. (Change *No one* to *Everybody*.)

2. All of the juice is sour. (Change *All* to *Most*.)

3. Nobody needs a ride. (Change *Nobody* to *Some of my friends*.)

4. One of the puppies has black ears. (Change *One* to *Many*.)

5. Several of the actors are talented and ambitious. (Change *Several* to *Each*.)

6. Most of the water is gone. (Change *water* to *strawberries*.)

7. Both of the dancers have learned the new steps. (Change *Both* to *None*.)

8. Are any of the papers torn? (Change *papers* to *paper*.)

9. Some of the bread tastes delicious. (Change *bread* to *pears*.)

10. Have all of the candidates spoken? (Change *all* to *either*.)

11. Is one of the bikes a twelve-speed? (Change *one* to *many*.)

12. Several of our players are over six feet tall. (Change *Several* to *Each*.)

13. All of the houses have been painted. (Change *houses* to *house*.)

14. Few in my family like skiing. (Change *Few* to *All*.)

15. Did anybody eat my casserole? (Change *anybody* to *somebody*.)

MODULE 5: AGREEMENT

COMPOUND SUBJECTS

A ***compound subject*** consists of two or more nouns or pronouns that are joined by a conjunction and have the same verb.

5g Subjects joined by *and* usually take a plural verb.

Compound subjects joined by *and* that name more than one person or thing always take plural verbs.

EXAMPLES **Denzel Washington** and **Charlize Theron** have been in many movies.
Corn, tomatoes, and **green peppers grow** in my garden.

Compound subjects that name only one person or one thing take a singular verb.

EXAMPLES My favorite **singer and dancer is** Ben Vereen. [one person]
Macaroni and cheese is a terrific meatless meal. [one thing]

5h Singular subjects joined by *or* or *nor* take a singular verb.

EXAMPLES **Roberto** or **Eleanora has** been elected.
Has neither your **brother** nor your **sister** arrived?

5i When a singular subject and a plural subject are joined by *or* or *nor*, the verb agrees with the subject nearer the verb.

EXAMPLES Neither my parents nor my **sister is** in the audience tonight.
Either Emma or her **parents are** baby-sitting for Dr. Aquino tonight.

EXERCISE 8 Selecting Verbs That Agree in Number with Their Subjects

In each of the following sentences, underline the verb or verb phrase in parentheses that agrees in number with its subject.

EX. 1. Brazil and Argentina (*is*, *are*) South American nations.

1. Either Katya or Marie (*is leading, are leading*) the parade tomorrow.
2. Both Sandy Koufax and Mariano Rivera (*has set, have set*) pitching records.
3. Neither the fruit nor the vegetables (*seems, seem*) ripe.
4. Either Anna Kendrick or Emma Stone (*is playing, are playing*) the role.
5. (*Is, Are*) beans or corn being served as a side dish?

6. Willie Nelson and she (*has recorded, have recorded*) a duet.
7. Either Japan or China (*is, are*) the site of the chess tournament finals.
8. (*Was, Were*) the director and star of the movie Tyler Perry?
9. Either the lead singer or all of the band members (*is, are*) accepting the award.
10. Neither the spark plugs nor the starter (*appears, appear*) damaged.

EXERCISE 9 Working With a Partner to Write Sentences Using Correct Subject-Verb Agreement

Working with a partner, make complete sentences of the compound subjects below. On your own paper, add correct verbs and any other words you might need.

EX. 1. Either the laser beam or the x-rays
1 . *Either the laser beam or X-rays were among the greatest discoveries.*

1. Radar and sonar
2. Either penicillin or aspirin
3. Neither Saturn nor Jupiter
4. Both fire and atomic energy
5. Science and industry
6. Neither a missile nor several rockets
7. The sliced tomatoes and the baked squash
8. Not only the computer disks but also the display terminals
9. Neither our science project nor theirs
10. Either the players or the captain

MODULE 5: AGREEMENT

COLLECTIVE NOUNS

5j Collective nouns may be either singular or plural.

A ***collective noun*** is singular in form, but it names a group of persons or things.

Collective Nouns			
army	club	group	series
assembly	committee	herd	squad
audience	crowd	jury	staff
band	faculty	majority	swarm
choir	family	number	team
class	flock	public	troop

Use a singular verb with a collective noun when you mean the group as a unit. Use a plural verb when you mean the members of the group as individuals.

EXAMPLES The choir **is** singing at today's assembly. [the choir as a unit]
The choir **are** helping each other to learn the new music. [the choir members as individuals]

EXERCISE 10 Writing Sentences with Collective Nouns

From the list above, select ten collective nouns. On your own paper, use each in a pair of sentences. Each pair of sentences should show how the collective noun may be singular and plural.

EX. 1. *a.* *The faculty meets every Thursday afternoon.*
b. *The faculty are comparing their different class schedules.*

MODULE 5: AGREEMENT

REVIEW EXERCISE 1

A. Selecting Verbs That Agree with Their Subjects

In each sentence below, underline the verb or verb phrase in parentheses that agrees in number with its subject.

EX. 1. Someone who has made many great movies (*is, are*) Al Pacino.

1. My aunt Kamaria often (*goes, go*) back to her birthplace in Africa.
2. Lima, along with Buenos Aires, (*has, have*) many beautiful buildings.
3. (*Does, Do*) the sandwiches in the picnic basket need to be refrigerated?
4. The cost of wool coats (*has risen, have risen*) recently.
5. Alicia Keys' ability as a musician, as well as her beautiful song lyrics, (*has made, have made*) her very popular.
6. Neither of the doctors (*is seeing, are seeing*) any patients today.
7. (*Has, Have*) most of the birds flown south for the winter?
8. None of the ink (*has stained, have stained*) the rug.
9. Either Sheila or Josh and Alan (*is holding, are holding*) a cast party.
10. The songwriter and singer whom I respect most (*is, are*) Stevie Wonder.

B. Proofreading For Subject-Verb Agreement

In each sentence below, underline any verbs that do not agree in number with their subjects. Then, on the line before the sentence, write the correct form of the verb. If a sentence contains no errors in subject-verb agreement, write *C* on the line.

EX. ___*is*___ 1. All of the paint in this store are on sale.

__________ 1. Most of the action scenes in the movie was exciting.

__________ 2. Has any of the bread turned stale?

__________ 3. The goat, along with the horses and sheep, have been in the pasture all day.

__________ 4. Volunteer jobs at the local hospital is plentiful.

__________ 5. Do either of your parents work in a factory?

MODULE 5: AGREEMENT

OTHER PROBLEMS IN AGREEMENT

5k A verb agrees with its subject, not with its predicate nominative.

SINGULAR My favorite **vegetable is peas.**
PLURAL **Peas are** my favorite **vegetable.**

5l When the subject follows the verb, make sure that the verb agrees with it.

In sentences beginning with *here* or *there* and in questions, the subject follows the verb.

SINGULAR Here **is** the **box** of napkins. PLURAL Here **are** the **napkins.**
SINGULAR Where **is** that **pair** of socks? PLURAL Where **are** those **socks?**

NOTE Contractions such as *here's, there's, how's*, and *what's* include the singular verb *is*. Use one of these contractions only if a singular subject follows it.

INCORRECT There's many cars on the road. [plural subject, singular verb]
SINGULAR **There's** a lot of **traffic** on the road.
PLURAL There **are** many **cars** on the road.

5m Words stating amounts usually take singular verbs.

EXAMPLES Two weeks **makes** a great vacation.
Five dollars **is** the price of a movie ticket.

5n The verb in a clause following the phrase *one of those* should be plural.

EXAMPLE *Aladdin* is **one of those** movies that **remain** popular for years.

5o *Every* or *many an* before a subject takes a singular verb.

EXAMPLES **Every** man and woman **is voting** today.
Many an athlete **improves** with the help of a coach.

5p Some nouns, although plural in form, take singular verbs. Such nouns may include the titles of works of art, literature, or music.

EXAMPLES **News** of the hurricane **has been reported** on television.
***Trees* is** a poem by the American author Joyce Kilmer.

A few nouns ending in *–ics* may be singular or plural.

EXAMPLES **Politics is** an interesting subject.
Your **politics were** the cause of the argument.

EXERCISE 11 Selecting Verbs That Agree in Number with Their Subjects

In each sentence below, underline the verb, phrase, or contraction in parentheses that agrees in number with its subject.

EX. 1. Velma is one of those singers who (*has, <u>have</u>*) natural talent.

1. Five years (*seems, seem*) a long time to be away from home.
2. Here (*is, are*) my collection of stamps.
3. The main ingredient in borscht, a Russian soup, (*is, are*) beets.
4. (*Where's, Where are*) the public swimming pool?
5. Every dog and cat at the city pound (*is, are*) available for adoption.
6. *The Three Sisters* (*is, are*) a play by the Russian playwright Anton Chekhov.
7. (*There's, There are*) nine planets in our solar system.
8. Many a young reader (*has, have*) enjoyed the books by Katherine Paterson.
9. Of all the local musical groups, Grupo Fantasma (*seems, seem*) the best, in my opinion.
10. Old Yeller was one of those fictional dogs that (*was, were*) always getting into trouble but still remained lovable.
11. An apple (*is, are*) one of those fruits that (*tastes, taste*) good raw.
12. Every plate in that cupboard (*has, have*) a chip on it.
13. My uncle's pumpkins (*win, wins*) a ribbon every year at the county fair.
14. Two cars (*fill, fills*) the work area in Mr. Kristan's garage.
15. (*How's, How are*) the weather in Florida?
16. (*Is, Are*) civics a good course to take?
17. This chain of stores (*sells, sell*) the best bread.
18. My favorite place (*is, are*) the mountains.
19. That sack of potatoes (*contain, contains*) the russet type of potatoes.
20. I am on a train that (*has, have*) two cabooses.

MODULE 5: AGREEMENT

REVIEW EXERCISE 2

A. Selecting Verbs That Agree in Number with Their Subjects

In each sentence below, underline the verb or phrase that agrees in number with its subject.

EX. 1. (*Here's*, *Here are*) a collection of poems by Gwendolyn Brooks.

1. *The Woman and the Men* (*is, are*) a book of poems by Nikki Giovanni.
2. News about the flood (*makes, make*) us very concerned.
3. Twenty dollars (*seems, seem*) too high a price for a CD.
4. Where (*does, do*) your parents shop for fresh vegetables?
5. (*There's, There are*) many pieces of broken glass on the sidewalk.
6. A popular German dish (*is, are*) sauerbraten and noodles.
7. *More Cricket Songs* (*is, are*) a collection of Japanese haiku poems translated and edited by Harry Behn.
8. (*Has, Have*) all of the firewood been burned?
9. Every singer and dancer in the production (*rehearses, rehearse*) in this hall.
10. *Hunted Mammals of the Sea* is one of those valuable books that (*describes, describe*) the problem of endangered animals.

B. Proofreading a Paragraph for Errors in Subject-Verb Agreement

In the following paragraph, draw a line through any verb that does not agree in number with its subject. Write the correct form of the verb in the space above the incorrect word. Some sentences may contain no errors in agreement.

enjoys
EX. [1] Many a young tennis player ~~enjoy~~ watching professional tennis matches.

[1] Gabriela Sabatini was one of those tennis players who played a strong game. [2] Her match against Steffi Graf in the U. S. Open proved her greatness as a competitor. [3] Sabatini, who is from Argentina, were giving Steffi Graf, the German tennis star, a hard match. [4] Here's the details from that match. [5] In the middle of

the second set, Graf, as well as most of the spectators, were sure that Sabatini would lose. [6] However, one of Sabatini's greatest strengths were volleys at the net. [7] Suddenly, Sabatini, not Graf, were playing very aggressive tennis. [8] What was the results of her aggressive playing? [9] She were successful in winning the last four games of the set! [10] Friendship and respect was evident between these two great players; and although Graf finally won the match in the third set, she was full of compliments for her talented rival.

C. Reporting on School Activities

You are the reporting secretary for the tenth grade at your school. You have been asked to report to the class president on the plans for the upcoming school talent show. Several clubs and organizations in the school have volunteered to help. On your own paper, write your report to the class president. Base your report on the details and notes listed below. Feel free to add your own ideas as well. Your report should contain ten sentences. Make sure that your report contains no errors in subject-verb agreement.

NOTES:

Ushers:	varsity cheerleaders and student council representatives
Music:	the honor band or the concert orchestra
Ticket sales:	Vocational Club or Spanish Club
Advertising:	school newspaper staff or Literary Club
Staging:	Drama Club or Debate Team
Master of ceremonies:	member of the Speech Club

EX. 1. *The varsity cheerleaders and three student council representatives have volunteered to be ushers for the performance.*

MODULE 5: AGREEMENT

PRONOUN AGREEMENT

The word that a pronoun refers to is called its ***antecedent.***

5q A pronoun should agree with its antecedent in gender and number.

Only the third-person singular pronouns indicate the gender of their antecedents. Masculine pronouns (*he, him, his*) refer to males; feminine pronouns (*she, her, hers*) refer to females; and neuter pronouns (*it, its*) refer to things and, often, to animals.

EXAMPLES Has **Cheryl** finished **her** report?
The **horse** was hungry, so I filled **its** bucket with oats.

When the antecedent of a personal pronoun is another kind of pronoun, determine the gender to use by looking at the phrase that follows the antecedent.

EXAMPLES **Neither** of the **men** has finished **his** work.
Each of the **girls** has brought **her** lunch.

When the antecedent could be either masculine or feminine, use both the masculine and feminine forms.

EXAMPLE **Each** of the **students** has finished **his or her** report.

NOTE You can often avoid the *his or her* construction by revising the sentence to use the plural form of the pronoun.
EXAMPLE **All** of the **students** have finished **their** reports.

(1) Use a singular pronoun to refer to the antecedent *each, either, neither, one, everyone, everybody, no one, nobody, anyone, anybody, someone,* or *somebody.* The use of a clause or phrase after the antecedent does not change the number of the antecedent.

EXAMPLES **Each** of the **birds** has made **its** nest.
Everyone who plays on the **girls'** tennis team has **her** own racket.

(2) Use a singular pronoun to refer to two or more singular antecedents joined by *or* or *nor.*

EXAMPLE Either **Jonas** or **William** will make **his** presentation next.

(3) Use a plural pronoun to refer to two or more antecedents joined by *and.*

EXAMPLE The **director** and the **stage manager** made the sets **themselves.**

EXERCISE 12 Selecting Pronouns That Agree with Their Antecedents

In each sentence below, fill in the blank with a pronoun or a pair of pronouns that agrees with the antecedent.

EX. 1. Each of the orchestra members has practiced *his or her* part.

1. Students who want to join the skating team should turn in _______________ registration forms.
2. Do both of the boys need _______________ schedules changed?
3. Marilyn and Sue designed the costumes _______________.
4. Has everyone in the apartment building put out _______________ trash?
5. Neither Phil nor Roberto has eaten _______________ lunch yet.
6. One calf had strayed from _______________ herd.
7. Two of the singers in the men's chorus have misplaced _______________ sheet music.
8. Nobody in my class rides _______________ bike to school anymore.
9. One of the men who works with us has gotten _______________ pay raise.
10. The treasurer and the secretary have filed _______________ reports.
11. Someone in the girls' school has called _______________ parents.
12. Each of my sisters has _______________ own workshop.
13. When she closed the door, it fell off _______________ hinges.
14. Both of her uncles brought _______________ presents to the wedding.
15. Either Mr. Petrakis or Mr. Villeré will read _______________ family history.
16. The bull got _______________ horns caught in a fence.
17. My mother washed _______________ car last Saturday.
18. All my uncles knit _______________ own sweaters.
19. The pig and the stallion escaped from _______________ pens.
20. Did you see the statue of Miss Lila Ogletree, the founder of our school? There's a pigeon sitting on _______________ nose.

MODULE 5: AGREEMENT

MODULE REVIEW

A. Proofreading Sentences for Subject-Verb and Pronoun-Antecedent Agreement

Proofread the sentences below for errors in subject-verb agreement and pronoun-antecedent agreement. Draw a line through any errors. Then, on the line before the sentence, write your correction. If a sentence contains no errors, write *C* on the line.

EX. _*has*_ 1. Many a wild horse ~~have~~ been trained to accept a saddle.

__________ 1. Each of the clubs has their own rules.

__________ 2. The coach and leading player were Gordie Howe.

__________ 3. All of the sportscasters have written their stories.

__________ 4. Sixty dollars seem too much to pay for a team jacket.

__________ 5. None of the fruit in the orchard were ripe.

__________ 6. Most of our neighbors grows flowers around their mailboxes.

__________ 7. Tanya, together with her sisters, were planning a party.

__________ 8. Every citizen must protect their civil rights.

__________ 9. Matt, not Cora and I, always wash the dishes after Sunday dinner.

__________ 10. Here's the directions to the Museum of African Culture.

B. Proofreading a Paragraph for Errors in Subject-Verb and Pronoun-Antecedent Agreement

In the following paragraph, draw a line through any errors in subject-verb agreement or pronoun-antecedent agreement. Write your correction in the space above the incorrect word. Some sentences may contain no agreement errors.

EX. [1] Joni Phelps, along with her sons Mike and Marty, ~~have~~ *has* climbed to the top of Mount McKinley.

[1] Joni Phelps is one of those women who knows what courage is all about. [2] Phelps, throughout her life, have enjoyed hikes and adventures. [3] However, Phelps lost their eyesight almost twenty-five years ago. [4] She has relied on a guide dog and his sense of sight ever since. [5] One winter, Phelps, together with her two grown sons,

were preparing for a dream come true. [6] They began lifting weights and practicing his rock-climbing skills. [7] All of the work were worth it. [8] Phelps, accompanied by her sons, were the first woman who is visually impaired to climb Mount McKinley, the tallest mountain in North America. [9] Anyone who has climbed Mount McKinley has had their own hardships with the sheer, rocky cliffs and the sudden snowstorms. [10] Many a climber have been forced to turn back, but not Joni, Mike, and Marty Phelps.

C. Creating a Time Capsule

You and your classmates are creating a time capsule to show people of the future what life was like during your time. Choose ten items you would like to leave in the time capsule. In the space below, identify each item, and explain why you chose it. Create two or more sentences for each item. Be sure to check your sentences for subject-verb agreement and pronoun-antecedent agreement.

EX. *A pennant from the team that won the last World Series seems like an interesting item for the time capsule. To many people I know, baseball is very important.*

MODULE 6: USING PRONOUNS CORRECTLY

CASE OF PRONOUNS

Case is the form of a noun or pronoun that shows how the word is used in a sentence. There are three cases: *nominative, objective*, and *possessive.*

Nouns have the same form in both the nominative and the objective case. For example, a noun used as a subject (nominative case) will have the same form when it is used as the object of a preposition (objective case). Nouns usually add an apostrophe and an *s* to form the possessive case.

NOMINATIVE CASE The **girl** dropped her book. [subject]

OBJECTIVE CASE Give the **girl** her book. [indirect object]

POSSESSIVE CASE This is the **girl's** book. [ownership]

Personal pronouns change form in the different cases.

CASE FORMS OF PERSONAL PRONOUNS		
Singular		
Nominative Case	**Objective Case**	**Possessive Case**
I	me	my, mine
you	you	your, yours
he, she, it	him, her, it	his, her, hers, its
Plural		
Nominative Case	**Objective Case**	**Possessive Case**
we	us	our, ours
you	you	your, yours
they	them	their, theirs

Notice that only *you* and *it* have the same form in the nominative and the objective case.

NOTE Some teachers prefer to call possessive pronouns, such as *my*, adjectives. Follow your teacher's directions in labeling possessive forms.

EXERCISE 1 Identifying Personal Pronouns and Their Cases

Identify the case of the italicized pronoun by writing *nom.* for *nominative, obj.* for *objective*, or *poss.* for *possessive* on the line before each sentence below.

EX. ___*poss.*___ 1. Stephen Hawking visited Seattle to talk about *his* new book.

_______ 1. Because of an illness, *he* communicated through a computer.

_______ 2. Stephen Hawking, one of the most famous scientists in the world, gave *his* speech from a wheelchair.

_______ 3. Several teenagers in his audience were sitting in *their* own wheelchairs.

_______ 4. Although Hawking had Lou Gehrig's disease, *he* continued to work both as a scientist and as an author.

_______ 5. His book, *A Brief History of Time*, has sold more than five million copies even though *its* topic is highly scientific.

_______ 6. Sean and *I*, as some of those Seattle teenagers, have read the book.

_______ 7. Hawking may have been more familiar to *them* from an appearance on the television program *Star Trek: The Next Generation.*

_______ 8. *They* would also have seen Albert Einstein and Sir Isaac Newton, famous scientists from the past, on that show.

_______ 9. The rerun of that episode was on last week and we watched *it.*

_______ 10. If that episode comes on again, please tell *us.*

_______ 11. Hawking's book is about *his* theories of black holes and new universes.

_______ 12. The book also gives information about *him* and his personal life.

_______ 13. Someone asked *him* why he wrote a book.

_______ 14. Using a computer voice, *he* said that he did it because he had to pay for his nurses.

_______ 15. What an amazing man *he* was!

_______ 16. The Seattle teenagers asked Hawking many questions about *his* daily life.

_______ 17. They wanted *him* to explain how he was able to communicate.

_______ 18. How did the computer screen that was attached to *his* wheelchair work?

_______ 19. Did *it* operate like an ordinary computer?

_______ 20. How much work on the keyboard did *he* have to do?

MODULE 6: USING PRONOUNS CORRECTLY

THE NOMINATIVE CASE

6a The subject of a verb is in the nominative case.

EXAMPLES **I** read the magazine. [*I* is the subject of *read.*]
Anne and **he** sang together. [*Anne* and *he* are the two parts of the compound subject of the verb *sang*.]
We hoped that **they** would win the contest. [*We* is the subject of *hoped*, and *they* is the subject of *would win*.]

If you are not sure which form of the pronoun to use in a compound subject, try each pronoun separately with the verb.

EXAMPLE (*Him, He*) and (*me, I*) waited for the bus.
Him waited for the bus. [incorrect use of objective case]
He waited for the bus. [correct use of nominative case]
Me waited for the bus. [incorrect use of objective case]
I waited for the bus. [correct use of nominative case]

ANSWER **He** and **I** waited for the bus.

6b A predicate nominative is in the nominative case.

A ***predicate nominative*** is a noun or pronoun that follows a linking verb and explains or identifies the subject of the sentence. A pronoun used as a predicate nominative always follows a form of the verb *be* or a verb phrase ending in *be* or *been*.

EXAMPLES The writer of that essay is **she**. [*She* follows the linking verb *is* and identifies the subject *writer*.]
The artist could have been **he.** [*He* follows the linking verb *could have been* and identifies the subject *artist*.]
The cocaptains of the team will be **she** and **I.** [*She* and *I* follow the linking verb *will be* and identify the subject *co-captains*.]

NOTE In casual conversation, expressions such as *It's me* and *That's her* are acceptable. Avoid them in more formal speaking situations, such as job interviews. In your written work, don't use them unless you are creating casual conversation in dialogue.

EXERCISE 2 Identifying Nominative Case Pronouns

For each of the following sentences, underline the correct personal pronoun in parentheses.

EX. 1. It may be (<u>*she*</u>, *her*) at the door.

1. The ride was long and boring, and (*I, me*) soon fell asleep.
2. Mrs. Olivero and (*her, she*) enjoy jogging together.
3. Mom thought that (*us, we*) should learn how to cook authentic Mexican dishes.
4. Ray suggested that he and (*I, me*) study together after school.
5. The person in charge of the project is (*he, him*).
6. Gloria and (*them, they*) signed up to work at the recycling center.
7. The winners of the tournament could be that team or (*we, us*).
8. Would you and (*she, her*) like to stay for dinner?
9. I think that you and (*me, I*) will be chosen to represent our class.
10. The last two people to sign up to learn Korean in the adult education class were my mother and (*her, she*).

EXERCISE 3 Proofreading for Correct Use of Nominative Case Pronouns

In the paragraph below, draw a line through each incorrect pronoun form. Write the correct pronoun in the space above the word. Some sentences are correct.

EX. [1] Karina and ~~me~~ (I) wanted to learn how to make pottery.

[1] Her and I signed up for a pottery-making class at the Borden Crafts Center. [2] Every Saturday morning, she and me bike over to the center. [3] Sylvia Chin is a well-known local potter, and it is her who teaches the class. [4] She and her husband also own a small pottery shop. [5] She makes the clay pottery; the sculptor of the porcelain is him. [6] Sylvia says Karina and me will soon be making beautiful bowls and cups. [7] Karina learns quickly and, in fact, the star of the class is her. [8] The one to worry about doing well should be me. [9] Ms. Chin says, "I think that you and me have something in common. [10] The first vase I ever made was mistaken for a cereal bowl."

MODULE 6: USING PRONOUNS CORRECTLY

THE OBJECTIVE CASE

6c Direct objects and indirect objects are in the objective case.

A ***direct object*** is a noun or pronoun that receives the action of the verb or shows the result of the action.

EXAMPLES The neighbor's dog followed **us** home. [*Us* tells *whom* the dog followed.]
Earline described **it** in perfect detail. [*It* tells *what* Earline described.]

An ***indirect object*** is a noun or pronoun that tells *to whom* or *for whom* the action of the verb is done.

EXAMPLES Miss Acosta gave **them** free passes to the science museum. [*Them* tells *to whom* Miss Acosta gave the passes.]
Hillary bought **her** the video. [*Her* tells *for whom* Hillary bought the video.]

To choose the correct pronoun in a compound direct object or compound indirect object, try each form of the pronoun separately in the sentence.

EXAMPLE The artist drew a sketch of her and (*me, I*).
The aritist drew *I*. [incorrect use of nominative case]
The artist drew *me*. [correct use of objective case]

ANSWER The artist drew a sketch of her and **me.**

EXAMPLE Julian sent them and (*we, us*) postcards.
Julian sent *we* postcards. [incorrect use of nominative case]
Julian sent *us* postcards. [correct use of objective case]

ANSWER Julian sent them and **us** postcards.

EXERCISE 4 Using Objective Case Pronouns

In each of the following sentences, write a personal pronoun on the line provided. Use a variety of pronouns. Do not use *you* or *it*.

EX. 1. The teacher gave ___*them*___ a surprise quiz.

1. Have you asked ____________ about the math assignment?
2. The committee will award ____________ an honorary prize.
3. After the auditions were over, the director picked ____________ to play the part of the shopkeeper.

4. Carlotta's mother offered ___________ and ___________ some helpful advice.
5. Tell ___________ three causes for the beginning of the Civil War.
6. The fire alarm startled ___________ .
7. Don't forget to mail Janine and ___________ their concert tickets.
8. Tranh showed ___________ and ___________ how to make a Vietnamese dessert called *banhit*.
9. Watching horror movies before bed sometimes gives ___________ nightmares.
10. A crowd of people pushed ___________ through the open doors.

EXERCISE 5 Proofreading Sentences for Correct Pronoun Case

In each of the sentences below, draw a line through any incorrect pronouns. On the line before the sentence, write the correct form of each pronoun. If a sentence contains no error in pronoun usage, write *C*.

EX. ___*him*___ 1. I showed Dad and ~~he~~ photographs from the trip.

___________ 1. Because of heavy traffic, the ride from the airport took Francie and I over an hour.

___________ 2. My uncle who lives in San Juan, Puerto Rico, invited us to spend part of the summer with him.

___________ 3. If this explanation confuses you and he, I'll repeat it in simpler terms.

___________ 4. The ending surprised he and I.

___________ 5. Who told you and she about what happened in science lab?

___________ 6. The reporter asked the other witnesses and I what had happened.

___________ 7. Dolores read he and me an excerpt from a book by one of her favorite writers, Amy Tan.

___________ 8. We waved when we spotted Maurice and they a few rows back.

___________ 9. Mrs. Barry paid me generously for baby-sitting the twins.

___________ 10. A monorail carried our parents and we across the amusement park.

MODULE 6: USING PRONOUNS CORRECTLY

OBJECTS OF PREPOSITIONS

6d The object of a preposition is in the objective case.

A prepositional phrase is a group of words consisting of a preposition, a noun or pronoun that serves as the object of the preposition, and any modifiers of that object.

EXAMPLES	from the **governor**	near **us**	behind the **door**
	to Tekla and **her**	in front of **them**	next to **him**

When the object of a preposition is compound, try each pronoun separately in the prepositional phrase.

EXAMPLE The report was prepared by (*he, him*) and (*I, me*).
The report was prepared by *he*. [incorrect use of nominative case]
The report was prepared by *him*. [correct use of objective case]
The report was prepared by *I*. [incorrect use of nominative case]
The report was prepared by *me*. [correct use of objective case]

ANSWER The report was prepared by **him** and **me.**

NOTE Using incorrect pronoun forms after the prepositions *between* and *for* is a common error. The pronouns should be in the objective case.

INCORRECT between you and *I*; for *he* and *they*
CORRECT between **you** and **me**; for **him** and **them**

EXERCISE 6 Choosing Correct Pronouns as Objects of Prepositions

In each of the following sentences, underline the correct pronoun in parentheses.

EX. 1. The photograph was of (*she, <u>her</u>*) and (*I, <u>me</u>*).

1. The director lost his temper and yelled at (*they, them*).
2. These letters just arrived for Shanti and (*I, me*).
3. According to (*he, him*), this is the way to Becky's house.
4. The dog jumped on the couch and squeezed between Lenny and (*he, him*).
5. After Val finished his biographical sketch of Harriet Tubman, he gave copies of it to (*we, us*) and (*he, him*).
6. The kite soared high above (*she, her*) and (*I, me*).

7. Six others are coming to the movie in addition to you and (*I, me*).
8. They were unaware that a giant snapping turtle was crawling behind (*he, him*) and (*she, her*).
9. Tómas handed a bowl of the paella that he had made for Spanish class to (*they, them*) and (*I, me*).
10. Who is standing in front of (*they, them*) and (*we, us*)?
11. Pilar wanted to know what her boss had said about (*she, her*).
12. During the earthquake, we heard the tinkling of glasses knocking together all around (*we, us*).
13. Ask Namka and (*he, him*) if they can wash the dishes today for Ben and (*I, me*).
14. The rabbit tried to make herself small when she saw the hawk hovering over (*she, her*).
15. What made you pour water onto (*they, them*) and (*we, us*)?

EXERCISE 7 Writing Sentences Using Pronouns as Objects of Prepositions

Write twenty sentences on your own paper, using each of the following prepositions with a personal pronoun as the object of the preposition. Include compound objects in at least four of your sentences. [Hint: You may want to refer to the charts of personal pronouns at the beginning of the module.]

EX. 1. without
1. *We left for school without James and her.*

1. with
2. behind
3. for
4. instead of
5. except
6. according to
7. between
8. toward
9. concerning
10. because of
11. against
12. over
13. near
14. in addition to
15. past
16. underneath
17. on account of
18. through
19. without
20. beside

MODULE 6: USING PRONOUNS CORRECTLY

REVIEW EXERCISE

A. Identifying Correct Pronoun Forms

In each of the sentences below, underline the correct pronoun in parentheses. On the line before the sentence, identify the pronoun's use in the sentence. Write *s.* for *subject, p.n.* for *predicate nominative, d.o.* for *direct object, i.o.* for *indirect object*, or *o.p.* for *object of the preposition.*

EX. ___*s.*___ 1. Will Maria and (*she, her*) leave early?

_______ 1. The teacher assigned (*we, us*) a report on the poetry of Gwendolyn Brooks.

_______ 2. Cynthia and (*she, her*) have been friends since kindergarten.

_______ 3. Is there any mail for (*he, him*) and (*I, me*)?

_______ 4. Olympic silver medal winner Sasha Cohen inspired João and (*she, her*) to take up ice-skating.

_______ 5. Are your sisters and (*they, them*) coming home for Thanksgiving?

_______ 6. It's (*he, him*) or (*she, her*) at the door.

_______ 7. The referee seemed to be against (*we, us*).

_______ 8. Did you send (*she, her*) and (*he, him*) invitations to the awards ceremony?

_______ 9. When Spanish explorers came to the Americas, (*they, them*) came in search of the legendary kingdom of Quivira.

_______ 10. The caller could have been Sadie or (*she, her*).

_______ 11. Brenda said, "I'll give (*she, her*) a piece of my mind."

_______ 12. Native Americans in the Northeast made birch canoes and used (*they, them*) for fishing.

_______ 13. I looked up Fred Gipson in a biographical dictionary and found it was (*he, him*) who wrote *Old Yeller*.

_______ 14. Marco thought the book on chess would turn (*he, him*) into a champion player.

_______ 15. The archaeologists at the Cahokia site in East St. Louis gave permission for (*we, us*) to visit the excavations.

B. Proofreading for Correct Pronouns

In the paragraph below, draw a line through each pronoun used incorrectly. In the space above it, write the correct form of the pronoun. Some sentences contain no errors.

EX. [1] She and ~~me~~ I were discussing the portrayal of teenagers in the media.

[1] Often, newspaper stories and television programs show we to be selfish and lazy. [2] Here is a true story that her and I heard that presents teenagers in a different light. [3] Six-year-old Hung Ho was on his way home from school in Modesto, California, when a German shepherd began chasing him. [4] The boy was so frightened that him screamed and ran out into the street. [5] Coming down the street and aimed right at he was an automobile. [6] At the time, fourteen-year-old Poeuth Pann was at his post as school crossing guard. [7] Without thinking about his own safety, Poeuth ran to Hung, and him grabbed the boy from the car's path. [8] It was him that also comforted Hung until the young boy stopped crying. [9] As a result of his actions, the American Automobile Association presented Poeuth with one of its highest awards, the School Safety Patrol Lifesaving Medal. [10] I don't know if I could have been so brave if that had been me.

C. Collaborating to Write a Space Log Entry

For the last few months, you and three partners have been stationed at the outpost on planet Dima. Working with two or three partners, create an update for your space log describing what the four of you have done during the past week. On your own paper, write twenty sentences that tell about your daily schedules, your food sources and living quarters, the plant and animal life on Dima, or any other features of your life at this outpost. Use five nominative case and five objective case pronouns in your sentences. Underline and label the pronouns *nom.* for *nominative* or *obj.* for *objective.*

EX. *Day 45. Yesterday, Charles joined me (obj.) to check out Sector 421. We (nom.) took our lunches with us (obj.), because we (nom.) weren't sure the people along our route would have food that they (nom.) could share with us (obj.).*

MODULE 6: USING PRONOUNS CORRECTLY

WHO *AND* WHOM

6e The use of *who* and *whom* in a subordinate clause depends on how the pronoun functions in the clause.

Nominative Case	who, whoever
Objective Case	whom, whomever

NOTE In spoken English, the use of *whom* is gradually dying out. These days, it is acceptable to begin any spoken question with *who* regardless of whether the nominative or objective form is grammatically correct. In writing, though, it is still important to distinguish between *who* and *whom.*

When you are deciding whether to use *who* or *whom* in a subordinate clause, follow these steps.

Step 1: Find the subordinate clause.

Step 2: Decide how the pronoun is used in the clause—as a subject, predicate nominative, direct object, indirect object, or object of a preposition.

Step 3: Determine the case of the pronoun according to the rules of standard English.

Step 4: Select the correct form of the pronoun.

EXAMPLE Did you know that Julio is the one (*who, whom*) saved seats for us?

Step 1: The subordinate clause is (*who, whom*) *saved seats for us*.

Step 2: In this clause, the pronoun is the subject of the verb *saved.*

Step 3: As a subject, the pronoun should be in the nominative case.

Step 4: The nominative form is *who*.

ANSWER Did you know that Julio is the one **who** saved the seats for us?

EXAMPLE Rosie is the one (*who, whom*) the judges selected.

Step 1: The subordinate clause is (*who, whom*) *the judges selected.*

Step 2: In this clause, the pronoun is the direct object of the verb *selected: The judges selected* (*who, whom*)?

Step 3: As a direct object, the pronoun should be in the objective case.

Step 4: The objective form is *whom*.

ANSWER Rosie is the one **whom** the judges selected.

Remember that no words outside the subordinate clause affect the case of the pronoun.

Frequently, *whom* is left out of a subordinate clause, but its function is understood.

EXAMPLE The woman (whom) I spoke to is my aunt. [*Whom* is understood to be the object of the preposition *to*.]

EXERCISE 8 Identifying the Use of *Who* and *Whom* in Subordinate Clauses

In each sentence below, underline the subordinate clause containing *who* or *whom*. On the line before each sentence, write how the relative pronoun (*who* or *whom*) is used in its own clause. Write *s.* for *subject, p.n.* for *predicate nominative, d.o.* for *direct object, i.o.* for *indirect object*, or *o.p.* for *object of the preposition*.

EX. *p.n.* 1. Do we know who the members are?

_______ 1. The people whom I read about are scientists.

_______ 2. These scientists, who belong to the Rapid Assessment Program, study specific areas of the world's rain forests.

_______ 3. Do you know who the leader of the group is?

_______ 4. The team leader is Ted Parker, who likes studying birds.

_______ 5. Do you know to whom the study of mammals is most interesting?

_______ 6. Louise Emmons, who spent her childhood in such places as Malaysia and Spain, studies mammals.

_______ 7. Team members gather the information for whoever needs it.

_______ 8. Some of the information is used to prove to those who live near the rain forest that laws should be passed to preserve the forest.

_______ 9. Those people take this information to lawmakers whom they trust to make new laws.

_______ 10. This action benefits everyone, especially those people for whom the forest is home.

MODULE 6: USING PRONOUNS CORRECTLY

OTHER PRONOUN PROBLEMS

6f Pronouns used as appositives should be in the same case as the word they refer to.

An ***appositive*** is a noun or pronoun used with another noun or pronoun to identify or explain it.

EXAMPLES The program speakers, **he** and **she,** should sit up front. [The pronouns are in the nominative case because they are in apposition with the subject *speakers*.]
He cooked enough food for three people, **her, him,** and **me.** [The pronouns are in the objective case because they are in apposition with the object of the preposition *people*.]

To figure out the correct form of a pronoun used as an appositive or with an appositive, read the sentence with only the pronoun.

EXAMPLES The woman offered the two boys, Paul and (*he, him*), a reward.
The woman offered he a reward. [incorrect]
The woman offered him a reward. [correct]
The woman offered the two boys, Paul and **him,** a reward.

(*We, Us*) friends went camping together.
Us went camping together. [incorrect]
We went camping together. [correct]
We friends went camping together.

EXERCISE 9 Identifying the Correct Pronouns

In each of the following sentences, underline the correct pronoun in parentheses.

EX. 1. Mom called (*we, <u>us</u>*) girls in to dinner.

1. Have you met the new students, Denise and (*they, them*)?
2. Her best friends, Miki and (*she, her*), are her most loyal companions.
3. The band dedicated their final song to the music teachers, Ms. Enzio and (*she, her*).
4. The dance academy sent two applicants, you and (*I, me*), acceptance letters.
5. Two people, Karl and (*he, him*), missed the bus.
6. James Berry's children's short story "Ajeemah and His Son" is a favorite of my younger sister Odessa and (*she, her*).
7. (*We, Us*) yearbook workers meet every Wednesday before school.

8. The magician demonstrated for (*we, us*) members of the audience how the trick was done.
9. Dad heard the three opera singers, Plácido Domingo, José Carreras and (*he, him*), in concert.
10. Last Sunday evening, (*we, us*) photo club members gathered to look at slides of Anna's trip to Guatemala.

6g After *than* or *as* introducing an incomplete construction, use the pronoun form that would be used if the construction were completed.

EXAMPLES I understand French better than **she** (understands French).
I understand French better than (I understand) **her.**
We visit the city as often as **they** (visit the city).
We visit the city as often as (we visit) **them.**

EXERCISE 10 Selecting Pronouns for Incomplete Constructions in Sentences

On your own paper, write the correct pronoun in parentheses for each of the following sentences. Also, write in parentheses the missing part of the incomplete construction. If a sentence may be completed in two different ways, write both completions.

EX. 1. I know Janet better than (*she, her*).
1. *she (knows Janet); (I know) her*

1. We argued about the answer more loudly than (*they, them*).
2. Did they talk about the incident as much as (*we, us*)?
3. I understood the meaning of the poem better than (*he, him*).
4. She watched the Native American dance exhibition longer than (*I, me*).
5. Joe ate more lunch than (*we, us*).
6. Ms. Belindo offered to pay Nancy more than (*we, us*).
7. Did Kai hand in her paper sooner than (*I, me*)?
8. I traveled to see Grandfather as often as (*they, them*).
9. Koko liked Mr. Hirata even less than (*she, her*).
10. Not many gardeners are as careful as (*she, her*).

MODULE 6: USING PRONOUNS CORRECTLY

INEXACT PRONOUN REFERENCE

6h A pronoun should always refer clearly to its antecedent.

(1) Avoid an ambiguous reference.

In an ***ambiguous reference,*** a pronoun can refer to more than one antecedent.

AMBIGUOUS Bob saw Andy on his way home. [Who was on his way home, Bob or Andy?]

CLEAR While Bob was on **his** way home, **he** saw Andy.

or

CLEAR While Andy was on **his** way home, Bob saw **him.**

(2) Be sure that each pronoun you use has a specific, stated antecedent.

Sometimes a writer will suggest a particular word or idea without stating it. A pronoun that refers to this unstated word or idea is said to have a ***weak reference*** to the antecedent.

WEAK When I'm ready to eat, I cook it quickly in the microwave. [*It* may refer to breakfast, lunch, dinner, or a snack. The writer suggests, but does not state, which one.]

CLEAR When I'm ready to eat **lunch,** I cook **it** quickly in the microwave.

WEAK Joy loves playing the piano and wants to study it in college. [*It* may refer to the unstated noun *music.*]

CLEAR Joy loves playing the **piano,** and she wants to study **music** in college.

In conversation, people often use the pronouns *it, they*, and *you* unnecessarily. In writing, be sure to avoid such ***indefinite reference*** errors.

INDEFINITE On the postcard, it has a place for your return address. [The pronoun *it* is not necessary to the meaning of the sentence.]

CLEAR The postcard has a place for your return address.

INDEFINITE On the television news program, they warned that there would be a severe thunderstorm. [The pronoun *they* is not necessary to the meaning of the sentence.]

CLEAR The television news program issued a severe thunderstorm warning.

NOTE Familiar expressions such as *it is raining, it's early*, and *it seems like* are correct even though they contain inexact pronoun references. The antecedents to these pronouns are commonly understood to be the weather, time, and so forth.

EXERCISE 11 Correcting Inexact Pronoun References

On your own paper, rewrite each of the following sentences, correcting the inexact pronoun reference.

EX. 1. Michael talked to Max while he was in the cafeteria.
1. *While Michael was in the cafeteria, he talked to Max.*

1. Sue saw Aretha while she was waiting at the bus stop.
2. After reading Rob's poem and Earl's essay, Ms. Cowens commended it.
3. Whenever I see a play, I want to be like that.
4. In the article about former professional basketball player Dikembe Mutombo, they talk about his childhood in Zaire.
5. Fish were jumping all over the lake, but I didn't catch it.

EXERCISE 12 Proofreading for Inexact Pronoun References

On your own paper, revise the paragraph below, correcting the inexact pronoun references. If a sentence contains no errors, make no changes.

EX. [1] The surgeon general advises the president on federal health policies, which is his main responsibility.
1. *The surgeon general's main responsibility is to advise the president on federal health policies.*

[1] In 1993, President Bill Clinton appointed a new surgeon general, and it was confirmed by the United States Senate. [2] Dr. Joycelyn Elders succeeded Dr. Antonia Novello, and she was this country's fifteenth surgeon general. [3] In her career as a medical doctor, she concentrated on children's diseases, studying their causes and why they got them. [4] Because Dr. Elders was especially interested in health issues related to children, as surgeon general she focused on it. [5] In this article about Dr. Elders, they say that Dr. Elders oversaw the 6,500 people who work for the Public Health Service. [6] The Public Health Service was originally created in 1798 to provide health benefits for merchant marines, which helps explain why today they wear the Navy-type uniforms. [7] Public Health Service workers also hold Navy ranks because of it. [8] One of the most famous surgeon generals was Dr. C. Everett Koop. [9] Dr. Koop was appointed by President Ronald Reagan, and he really enjoyed wearing his admiral's uniform. [10] Dr. Koop worked hard to educate Americans about the dangers of smoking, and it declined because of this.

MODULE 6: USING PRONOUNS CORRECTLY

MODULE REVIEW

A. Correcting Pronoun Forms in Sentences

In each sentence below, draw a line through the incorrect pronoun form. On the line before the sentence, write the correct form of the pronoun. If the sentence contains no errors, write *C*.

EX. ___*she*___ 1. Ben and ~~her~~ went to the movies together.

_______ 1. We asked whom the stranger was.

_______ 2. Can you make up song lyrics as well as him?

_______ 3. Halfway through the race, the leaders were Angie, Marty, and her.

_______ 4. Sitting right in front of Josh and I was the actor Denzel Washington.

_______ 5. Do you and her disagree about everything?

_______ 6. Aki demonstrated her karate skills to Melissa, Paula, and I.

_______ 7. The coach asked her and me to work with the new players.

_______ 8. This year, there will be two band leaders, Elena and him.

_______ 9. Who do you think will be elected mayor next month?

_______ 10. Karla is a good artist, and no one draws better than her.

B. Proofreading a Paragraph for Correct Pronoun Forms

In the following paragraph, draw a line through each incorrect pronoun form. In the space above it, write the correct form of the pronoun. Some sentences may contain no errors.

We
EX. [1] ~~Us~~ students believed we could make things better.

[1] On our way home from school every day, a group of we students would walk past a vacant lot that was overgrown with weeds and littered with bottles, cans, and other trash. [2] Tanya and me would always comment about how awful the place looked and how someone should clean it up. [3] One day Nat, who likes to tease me, said, “You two, her and you, should clean it up if it bothers you so much.” [4] At first I just gave him one of my looks that said, “Who do you think you’re talking to?”

[5] Then Tanya said that maybe Nat was actually talking smarter than us for a change. [6] So, for the next six weeks, her and I showed up at the vacant lot every Saturday morning in our work clothes. [7] Nat came, too, with his older brother, and you wouldn't believe what hard workers they were. [8] Our parents gave us some trash bags and rubber gloves. [9] Before us kids knew it, the weeds and litter were gone, and the place was cleaned up. [10] The neighbors, all of who were happy about the change, discussed how to keep the lot clean. [11] Whomever suggested that it be used for community gardens had a good idea, I thought. [12] But Mr. Itoh said nothing uses more water than them, and the lot doesn't have running water. [13] Then, some local merchants who we are friendly with donated trees and bushes, some grass seed, two park benches, and lights. [14] Of course, the gifts meant more work for we kids. [15] That vacant lot is now a pretty park, and no one could be prouder than us.

C. Writing a Report on a Music Video

You are the director of a music video for the new song called "Life on the Edge." You have been asked to write a report to the producer to explain your ideas for the video.

Decide which singers, dancers, and musicians you will cast in your video. Their names may be fictitious or real. On your own paper, write fifteen sentences about the performers and the set. Include information about the performers' roles in the video. In ten of the sentences, use a different pronoun. Be sure all pronouns have clear, definite antecedents.

EX. *Video Report: Ziggy Marley would use his talent in Jamaican music to set the rhythm. I think we should light the set to make it look like the sun is shining.*

MODULE 7: USING VERBS CORRECTLY

REGULAR VERBS

7a The four principal parts of a verb are the *base form*, the *present participle*, the *past*, and the *past participle*.

Base Form	Present Participle	Past	Past Participle
start	(is) starting	started	(have) started
use	(is) using	used	(have) used

NOTE When the present participle and past participle forms are used as main verbs in sentences, they always require helping verbs.

7b A *regular verb* forms its past and past participle by adding *–d* or *–ed* to the base form.

Base Form	Present Participle	Past	Past Participle
cook	(is) cooking	cooked	(have) cooked
share	(is) sharing	shared	(have) shared
offer	(is) offering	offered	(have) offered
slip	(is) slipping	slipped	(have) slipped

NOTE A few regular verbs have an alternate past form ending in *–t*. For example, the past form of *dream* is *dreamed* or *dreamt*.

EXERCISE 1 Using Correct Verb Forms

In each of the following sentences, write the correct form of the verb given.

EX. 1. *learn* Most people have *learned* new computer skills.

1. *call* Have you ________________ the doctor?
2. *praise* Critics are ________________ the new book.
3. *risk* Carlos ________________ losing the race when he tripped.
4. *carry* She is ________________ a heavy load in her backpack.
5. *advertise* We usually ________________ our fall crafts show on the radio.
6. *play* The band is ________________ my favorite song.
7. *burn* The old house ________________ to the ground.

8. *recycle* The Fosters always ________________ their newspapers.

9. *cook* He has ________________ Vietnamese food for us several times.

10. *decide* After a long time, the judges ________________ on the winner of the debate.

11. *jump* Everyone ________________ into the pool when the whistle blew.

12. *watch* At the International Dance Festival, we ________________ the dancers from Mexico.

13. *drown* Several people ________________ in the flood.

14. *dream* Lee is ________________ of visiting his grandparents in Hong Kong.

15. *attack* We were ________________ by mosquitoes.

16. *play* Sam and Robin have been ________________ tennis for three hours.

17. *walk* Last Sunday afternoon we ________________ around Monument Valley.

18. *happen* What ________________ to the rest of the visitors?

19. *climb* The team from South Korea is ________________ the highest peak in South America.

20. *hope* I ________________ my aunt will show us the musical instruments she brought back from Africa.

21. *sell* Today, print newspapers do not usually ________________ as well as online subscriptions.

22. *include* This state park ________________ ponds, campsites, and an excellent bicycle path.

23. *offer* In the past, the book club ________________ a fifteen-percent discount to all its members.

24. *march* After we ate a picnic lunch, we ________________ in the Thanksgiving Day parade.

25. *boil* Eric, is the soup still ________________?

MODULE 7: USING VERBS CORRECTLY

IRREGULAR VERBS

7c An *irregular verb* forms its past and past participle in some other way than by adding *–d* or *–ed* to the base form.

Base Form	Past	Past Participle
break	broke	(have) broken
begin	began	(have) begun

NOTE When you are not sure whether a verb is regular or irregular, check a dictionary that lists the principal parts of irregular verbs.

COMMON IRREGULAR VERBS			
Base Form	**Present Participle**	**Past**	**Past Participle**
begin	(is) beginning	began	(have) begun
bite	(is) biting	bit	(have) bitten *or* bit
blow	(is) blowing	blew	(have) blown
break	(is) breaking	broke	(have) broken
bring	(is) bringing	brought	(have) brought
build	(is) building	built	(have) built
burst	(is) bursting	burst	(have) burst
catch	(is) catching	caught	(have) caught
choose	(is) choosing	chose	(have) chosen
come	(is) coming	came	(have) come
cost	(is) costing	cost	(have) cost
do	(is) doing	did	(have) done
draw	(is) drawing	drew	(have) drawn
drink	(is) drinking	drank	(have) drunk
drive	(is) driving	drove	(have) driven
eat	(is) eating	ate	(have) eaten
fall	(is) falling	fell	(have) fallen
feel	(is) feeling	felt	(have) felt
freeze	(is) freezing	froze	(have) frozen
get	(is) getting	got	(have) gotten *or* got

COMMON IRREGULAR VERBS			
Base Form	**Present Participle**	**Past**	**Past Participle**
give	(is) giving	gave	(have) given
go	(is) going	went	(have) gone
grow	(is) growing	grew	(have) grown
hurt	(is) hurting	hurt	(have) hurt
know	(is) knowing	knew	(have) known
lead	(is) leading	led	(have) led
lend	(is) lending	lent	(have) lent
lose	(is) losing	lost	(have) lost
make	(is) making	made	(have) made
meet	(is) meeting	met	(have) met
put	(is) putting	put	(have) put
ride	(is) riding	rode	(have) ridden
ring	(is) ringing	rang	(have) rung
run	(is) running	ran	(have) run
say	(is) saying	said	(have) said
see	(is) seeing	saw	(have) seen
sell	(is) selling	sold	(have) sold
send	(is) sending	sent	(have) sent
shrink	(is) shrinking	shrank	(have) shrunk
sing	(is) singing	sang	(have) sung
sink	(is) sinking	sank	(have) sunk
speak	(is) speaking	spoke	(have) spoken
stand	(is) standing	stood	(have) stood
steal	(is) stealing	stole	(have) stolen
swim	(is) swimming	swam	(have) swum
swing	(is) swinging	swung	(have) swung
take	(is) taking	took	(have) taken
tell	(is) telling	told	(have) told
throw	(is) throwing	threw	(have) thrown
wear	(is) wearing	wore	(have) worn
win	(is) winning	won	(have) won
write	(is) writing	wrote	(have) written

EXERCISE 2 Using the Correct Past and Past Participle Forms of Verbs

For each of the sentences below, write the correct form of the verb given.

EX. 1. *say* Lily ___*said*___ she is going to the folk-dancing class.

1. *sing* Before the game started, the players _______________ the National Anthem.
2. *write* My neighbor has _______________ a book about American Indian crafts.
3. *see* We _______________ the exhibit of moon rocks at the Museum of Science.
4. *steal* The runner just _______________ second base.
5. *freeze* The pond hasn't _______________ yet this winter.
6. *go* Manuel _______________ to Mexico to visit his aunt.
7. *make* Have you _______________ your costume for the parade?
8. *eat* Yoshi said that when he lived in Japan they _______________ a lot of fish.
9. *blow* The wind has _______________ down several power lines.
10. *sink* The *Titanic* _______________ after it hit an iceberg.
11. *take* We _______________ our boat out today for the first time this season.
12. *win* Do you know who _______________ the 2007 World Series?
13. *sell* Dexter has _______________ his old guitar so that he can buy a new one.
14. *wear* Last night, we had a good laugh looking at the pictures of the clothes my parents _______________ when they were young.
15. *tell* Dad _______________ everyone that dinner was ready.
16. *lend* Six weeks ago, Craig _______________ me his skis.
17. *ring* Last night, the church bells _______________ for five minutes.
18. *stand* The tourists have _______________ in line for hours, waiting to enter the museum.
19. *drink* The children _______________ all the cider.
20. *grow* These yellow roses are the most fragrant we have ever _______________.

EXERCISE 3 Using the Correct Past or Past Participle Forms of Verbs

In each of the sentences below, underline the correct form of the verb in parentheses.

EX. 1. Last night we (<u>*went*</u>, *gone*) to the State Fair.

1. Have you (*chose, chosen*) a topic for your report?
2. The Ashanti woman (*wore, worn*) a cloth called "kente."
3. Lani (*broke, broken*) open the coconut to drink the milk.
4. People have (*swam, swum*) in that lake for many years.
5. In Mali, farmers have (*build, built*) stone walls on the sides of mountains to hold the soil in place where they grew their crops.
6. Sarah had never (*drank, drunk*) Japanese green tea.
7. The carolers (*rang, rung*) bells as they sang.
8. Congresswoman Peters has (*rode, ridden*) in that parade every year.
9. Every year for the last ten years, Mr. Goldstein has (*ran, run*) in the Boston Marathon.
10. As a result of whaling, the number of whales in the ocean has (*shrank, shrunk*).
11. I (*saw, seen*) a copy of that poster at the museum store.
12. Because he was late getting home, Joe has not yet (*began, begun*) his homework.
13. During the heavy wind last night, the old maple tree (*fell, fallen*).
14. "This year on my birthday, I (*gave, given*) a new book to the library," Sharell said.
15. The one act-play (*wrote, written*) by my drama teacher drew a large audience at the festival.
16. The movie was the best science-fiction film we have (*saw, seen*).
17. On her trip to Utah, Elaine (*took, taken*) more than thirty pictures.
18. "The juice is sweet," said Paul, after he (*bit, bitten*) into the orange.
19. After the architect has (*drew, drawn*) the plans for the new house, the contractor will begin.
20. We cannot skate on the pond until the ice has (*froze, frozen*).

MODULE 7: USING VERBS CORRECTLY

VERB TENSE

7d The *tense* of a verb indicates the time of the action or state of being expressed by the verb.

(1) The *present tense* is used to express an action or a state of being occurring now, at the present time.

EXAMPLES She **runs** every day.
Are we **working** together? [progressive form]

The present tense is also used to express a general truth—something that is true all the time.

EXAMPLES Peace **walks** with freedom. The early bird **gets** the worm.

The present tense is often used in discussing literary works, particularly to summarize the plot or subject of a work. This use of the present tense is called the ***literary present***.

EXAMPLE In *Jane Eyre*, a poor orphan **takes** a job as a governess in a mysterious house.

(2) The *past tense* is used to express an action or a state of being that occurred in the past but does not continue into the present.

EXAMPLES He **opened** the door.
Was Herbert **working** with you? [progressive form]

(3) The *future tense* is used to express an action or a state of being that will occur in the future. It is formed with *will* or *shall*.

EXAMPLES She **will work** harder. **Shall** I **answer** the phone?

(4) The *present perfect tense* is used to express an action or a state of being that occurred at an indefinite time in the past. It is formed with *have* or *has*.

EXAMPLE Johnette **has** not **visited** us recently.

(5) The *past perfect tense* is used to express an action or a state of being that was completed before some other past action or event took place. It is formed with *had*.

EXAMPLE After they **had eaten** supper, they washed the dishes.

(6) The *future perfect tense* is used to express an action or a state of being that will be completed before some future action or event takes place. It is formed with *shall have* or *will have*.

EXAMPLE By the end of the year, I **will have run** in seventeen races.

For each tense another form, the ***progressive form,*** may be used to show continuing action. The progressive form is made up of a form of *be* plus the verb's present participle.

Form	Examples
Present Progressive	am, are, is running
Past Progressive	was, were running
Future Progressive	will (shall) be running
Present Perfect Progressive	has, have been running
Past Perfect Progressive	had been running
Future Perfect Progressive	will (shall) have been running

EXERCISE 4 Identifying Verb Tenses

In each sentence below, identify the tense and form of the verb. Write the answers on your own paper.

EX. 1. In the lecture series, Native Americans are sharing their ideas on political issues.
1. *present progressive*

1. Julia discovered the game of baseball at age eight.
2. Within hours, Caroline was boarding a plane to Washington, D.C.
3. The German shepherd and its owner rescue people in trouble.
4. Don has been broadcasting the news for the past five years.
5. How long will you remain in major league baseball?
6. By the end of this trip, we will have been traveling for six weeks straight.
7. Jocelyn had been planning to spend the weekend at Elaine's.
8. The train is running late this morning.
9. All the pipes in the neighborhood had frozen in the night.
10. Chicago and his brother are riding their horses today.
11. A robin has made a nest outside my window.
12. All this month, our class will be studying the South Pacific.
13. I write in my journal every night.
14. According to reports, the rain will have stopped by morning.
15. Had they been waiting long?

EXERCISE 5 Using the Different Tenses and Forms of Verbs in Sentences

In each of the following sentences, change the tense and form of the verb according to the directions given after the sentence.

EX. 1. She visited Chicago. (Change to present perfect.)

She has visited Chicago.

1. Elena lived in Costa Rica for a year. (Change to present perfect.)

____

2. After he revised his research paper, he typed it. (Change *revised* to past perfect.)

____

3. We rehearsed the play. (Change to present progressive.)

____

4. What happened in the story? (Change to present perfect progressive.)

____

5. After five o'clock, the mariachi band will play for an hour. (Change to future perfect progressive.)

____

6. The Apache performers were preparing for the Sunrise Dance. (Change to present perfect progressive.)

____

7. The plane arrives on time. (Change to future.)

____

8. The Inuit people developed ways to survive in the frozen Arctic regions. (Change to present perfect.)

____

9. Martha will start her science project by this afternoon. (Change to future perfect.)

____

10. Julian studies Spanish. (Change to past.)

____

11. We talked about the Aztec civilization. (Change to past perfect progressive.)

____

12. I read a book about African traditions, called *Ashanti to Zulu*. (Change to past progressive.)

____

13. Josie has been practicing every day. (Change to present.)

____

14. The tourists will visit Mesa Verde first. (Change to future progressive.)

____

15. Joseph Campbell collected myths from all over the world. (Change to present perfect.)

____

16. Toni Morrison wrote a new book. (Change to past perfect.)

____

17. We invited Inga to sing at the program. (Change to present perfect progressive.)

____

18. Before the day is over, I will have found my keys. (Change *will have found* to future.)

____

19. Cecilia will leave for Guatemala this week. (Change to future progressive.)

____

20. Have they gone to the Harvest Festival? (Change to future.)

____

MODULE 7: USING VERBS CORRECTLY

CONSISTENCY OF TENSE

7e Do not change needlessly from one tense to another.

NONSTANDARD Kam puts on her glasses and read the letter while everyone watched her.

STANDARD Kam **put** on her glasses and **read** the letter while everyone **watched** her. [The verbs are all in past tense.]

STANDARD Kam **puts** on her glasses and **reads** the letter while everyone **watches** her. [The verbs are all in present tense.]

NOTE Sometimes, to show a sequence of events, you will need to mix verb tenses.

EXAMPLE Before the class was over, we had heard several wonderful legends from the storyteller and now we will begin writing our own stories.

EXERCISE 6 Proofreading Paragraphs for Consistent Verb Tenses

In the following paragraphs, draw a line through each incorrect verb form. In the space above the verb, write the form of the verb that will make the verbs in the paragraph consistent in tense. Some sentences may be correct.

EX. [1] Rachel Carson was a marine biologist who ~~writes~~ *wrote* in a poetic manner about the world around her.

[1] Rachel Carson, who was an important figure in the movement to protect the environment, first become known for her books about the sea. [2] It must have surprised some people that she wrote about the ocean, because she grows up in western Pennsylvania, hundreds of miles from the sea. [3] As a girl, she showed a talent for writing and is interested in exploring the outdoors. [4] She wins a scholarship to the Pennsylvania College for Women, and there she struggled to decide whether to be a writer or a biologist. [5] She said she didn't realize that she could combine her two interests.

[6] She plans to become a college teacher. [7] Then she has decided to do some advanced studies. [8] She spends two summers working at the Woods Hole Marine

Biological Laboratory on Cape Cod in Massachusetts. [9] This is where Ms. Carson has come to know the sea. [10] She has decided her future work must involve the ocean.

[11] When she has finished her studies, she tried writing short pieces about the ocean for newspapers. [12] She needed, however, a reliable source of income to support her mother and her two orphaned nieces. [13] She finds a job writing about the ocean for a U.S. government radio program planned by the Bureau of Fisheries, part of the Department of the Interior. [14] The program is called "Romance Under the Waters," and Ms. Carson was paid $19.25 a week to write for it. [15] After she had been working several years for the government, she publishes an essay called "Undersea." [16] Her vivid descriptions of the ocean had caught the attention of the public. [17] She goes on to write a book, *Under the Sea Wind.* [18] It has been published during World War II and was, for the most part, unnoticed. [19] During the war, she continues to write for the government, working long hours as an editor in chief of publications. [20] When the war is over, she published a second book about the ocean, *The Sea Around Us.* [21] This book has been a best seller. [22] Perhaps her most important book, *Silent Spring* is published in 1962. [23] In it, Ms. Carson has warned about the effects of DDT, a chemical that was being widely used then to kill mosquitoes and other insects. [24] DDT is discovered to be harmful to humans and the environment. [25] At this time, people are not as concerned about protecting the environment, and *Silent Spring* help inspire new efforts to protect the earth.

MODULE 7: USING VERBS CORRECTLY

ACTIVE VOICE AND PASSIVE VOICE

7f A verb in the *active voice* expresses an action performed *by* its subject. A verb in the *passive voice* expresses an action done *to* its subject.

ACTIVE VOICE The tornado **uprooted** several large trees. [The subject, *tornado*, performs the action.]

PASSIVE VOICE Several large trees **were uprooted** by the tornado. [The subject, *trees*, receives the action.]

NOTE In a passive sentence, the verb phrase always includes a form of *be* and the past participle of the main verb. Other helping verbs may also be included.

ACTIVE VOICE She **raises** cattle on her farm.

PASSIVE VOICE Cattle **are being raised** on her farm.

The passive voice emphasizes the person or thing receiving the action rather than the person or thing performing the action. The passive voice is useful when the performer is difficult to identify, when you don't know who performed an action, or when you don't want to give away the performer's identity.

EXAMPLES The plan **was endorsed** both by public officials and local residents. [The performer is difficult to identify.]

She **was sent** an anonymous letter. [The performer is unknown.]

The flowers **were put** on Ms. Ortega's desk when she wasn't looking. [The performer is deliberately concealed.]

NOTE In most cases, you should avoid the passive voice. The active voice will make your writing much more direct and forceful.

EXERCISE 7 Identifying Sentences in the Active or Passive Voice

Identify each of the following sentences as *active* or *passive*. On the line before each sentence, write *act.* for *active* or *pass.* for *passive*.

EX. *act.* 1. Ruth is lighting the candles.

_______ 1. The tapes have been erased.

_______ 2. Many buildings in Los Angeles were damaged by the earthquake.

_______ 3. Lin wrote a skit for the program.

_______ 4. In Ghana, the people celebrate a Yam Festival to mark the beginning of their new year.

_______ 5. The generous contributions to the relief fund were appreciated.

_______ 6. The Hopi dancers performed their traditional Snake Dance.

_______ 7. A huge storm is forming off the coast of Alaska.

_______ 8. The votes were recounted carefully.

_______ 9. Raoul is going to the market.

_______ 10. Cecilia has been named captain of the team.

_______ 11. The band performed in the half-time show.

_______ 12. The refreshments were provided by volunteers.

_______ 13. Tomás is giving guitar lessons on Tuesdays.

_______ 14. Annie Oakley was born in 1860.

_______ 15. The earth is orbited by the moon.

EXERCISE 8 Using Verbs in the Active Voice and the Passive Voice

Study this illustration of an invention designed to help you wake up in the morning. Then write five sentences to describe the invention. Use both the active voice and the passive voice. After each sentence, write *act.* for *active* or *pass.* for *passive*.

EX. 1. *The sleeping person is being wakened by a ringing bell.* (*pass.*)

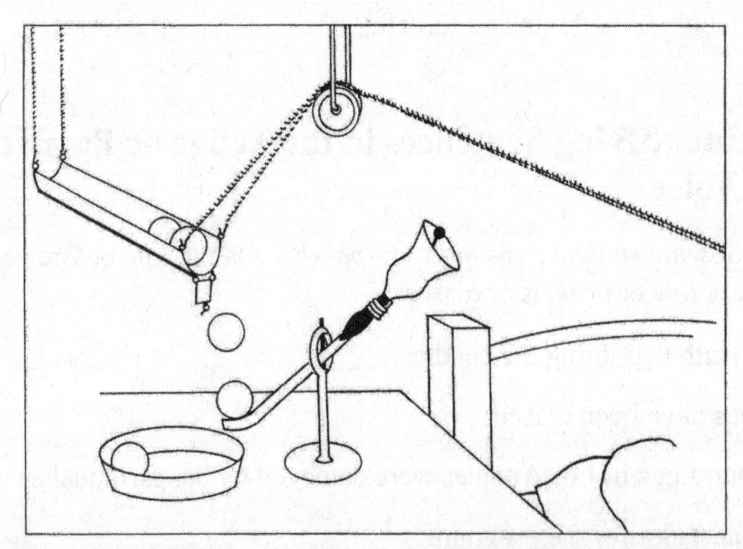

MODULE 7: USING VERBS CORRECTLY

LIE *AND* LAY

7g The verb *lie* means "to rest," "to recline," or "to remain in a lying position." *Lie* never takes an object. The verb *lay* means "to put (something) in a place." *Lay* usually takes an object.

Base Form	Present Participle	Past	Past Participle
lie (to rest)	(is) lying	lay	(have) lain
lay (to put)	(is) laying	laid	(have) laid

To decide whether to use *lie* or *lay*, ask yourself two questions:

Question 1: What do I want to say? Is the meaning "to be in a lying position" or "to put something down"?

Question 2: What time does the verb express, and which principal part accurately shows this time?

EXAMPLE The puppy has (*laid, lain*) there for an hour.

Question 1: **Meaning?** The meaning here is "to be in a lying position." Therefore, the verb should be *lie*.

Question 2: **Principal part?** The time is past, and the sentence requires the past participle with *have*. The past participle of *lie* is *lain*.

ANSWER The puppy **has lain** there for an hour.

EXAMPLE Maria (*lay, laid*) her books on the table.

Question 1: **Meaning?** The meaning here is "to put." Therefore, the verb should be *lay*.

Question 2: **Principal part?** The time is past and requires the past form, which is *laid*.

ANSWER Maria **laid** her books on the table.

EXERCISE 9 Identifying the Correct Forms of *Lie* and *Lay*

In each of the following sentences, underline the correct form of *lie* or *lay*.

EX. 1. The cat is (<u>*lying*</u>, *laying*) in the sun.

1. Israel (*lies, lays*) between Egypt and Jordan.

2. Akio (*lay, laid*) his shoes outside the door.

3. She didn't answer the doorbell because she was (*lying, laying*) down.

4. They have had to (*lie, lay*) a new floor in the library because of the flood.
5. That street sign has (*lain, laid*) on its side all day.
6. The newspaper is (*lying, laying*) in a puddle.
7. Please (*lie, lay*) the parcel on the table.
8. On the table, they (*lay, laid*) the food for the Harvest Festival.
9. The Khyber Pass (*lies, lays*) in rugged territory in Afghanistan.
10. The workers (*lay, laid*) down in the shade for a rest.

EXERCISE 10 Proofreading for the Correct Use of *Lie* and *Lay*

For each sentence below, underline the error. Then, on the line before each sentence, write the form of *lie* or *lay* that should appear in the sentence. If a sentence contains no errors, write *C* on the line.

EX. ___*lain*___ 1. The children have <u>laid</u> down for a nap.

______________ 1. The old books have laid in the attic for many years.

______________ 2. Will you lie the package on the counter?

______________ 3. Carmen couldn't tell from the map where the entrance to the cave lay.

______________ 4. In the afternoon, everyone laid down for a siesta.

______________ 5. The peddler lay his wares on a carpet by the roadside.

______________ 6. The dog is laying in the warmest spot in the house.

______________ 7. The Andes lay in South America.

______________ 8. We chose the route that laid to the west.

______________ 9. Olga has laid the cups all around the samovar.

______________ 10. His thoughts laid miles away.

______________ 11. Lori said, "Please lay the baby in his crib."

______________ 12. The carpenter has lain the hammer on the bench.

______________ 13. Thick fog laid over the harbor.

______________ 14. Why did you lie in bed so long?

______________ 15. Dust was laying everywhere in the room.

MODULE 7: USING VERBS CORRECTLY

SIT *AND* SET *AND* RISE *AND* RAISE

SIT AND *SET*

7h **The verb *sit* means "to rest in a seated position." *Sit* almost never takes an object. The meaning of the verb *set* is "to place" or "to put (something)." *Set* usually takes an object. Notice that *set* does not change form in the past or the past participle.**

Base Form	Present Participle	Past	Past Participle
sit (to rest)	(is) sitting	sat	(have) sat
set (to put)	(is) setting	set	(have) set

EXAMPLES I'll **sit** in the front row. [*Sit* takes no object.]
I'll **set** your papers here. [*Set* what? *Papers* is the object.]

EXERCISE 11 Writing the Forms of *Sit* and *Set*

In each sentence below, write the correct form of *sit* or *set* on the line provided.

EX. 1. Please ___*sit*___ here, Ms. Garcia.

1. Isabel ____________ in the second balcony.
2. My aunt ____________ the appetizers on the table.
3. That bird has been ____________ on the windowsill for hours.
4. We ____________ around the campfire, telling stories.
5. David ____________ the lit menorah in the window.
6. Felicity has ____________ out the plants in her garden.
7. They had to ____________ their experiment in the sunlight.
8. Lillian has ____________ here for an hour.
9. The Hopi participants ____________ out the gifts that are an important part of the Niman Dance.
10. Did you know there is a package ____________ on the steps?

RISE* AND *RAISE

7i **The verb *rise* means "to go up" or "to get up." *Rise* never takes an object. The verb *raise* means "to lift up (something)" or "to cause (something) to raise." *Raise* usually takes an object.**

Base Form	Present Participle	Past	Past Participle
rise (to get up)	(is) rising	rose	(have) risen
raise (to lift up)	(is) raising	raised	(have) raised

EXAMPLES Please **rise** from your seats to greet your guest. [*Rise* takes no object.]
Please **raise** your hand if you have a question. [*Raise* what? *Hand* is the object.]

EXERCISE 12 Writing the Forms of *Rise* and *Raise*

In each sentence below, write the correct form of *rise* or *raise* on the line provided.

EX. 1. The full moon is ___*rising*___.

1. The temperature ____________ in the afternoon.
2. The Himalayas ____________ between the plateau of Tibet and the plains of India.
3. Matthew's job is to ____________ the curtain before each set.
4. Tanya ____________ to ask a question.
5. To make piroshki, you need to let the dough ____________.
6. The woman walked to the window and ____________ the blinds.
7. The price of gasoline has ____________ this summer.
8. The audience ____________ to applaud the speaker.
9. We are trying to ____________ money to build an animal rescue center.
10. The students' interest in Mary McLeod Bethune has ____________ since we started studying her life.

MODULE 7: USING VERBS CORRECTLY

MODULE REVIEW

A. Writing Sentences Using the Correct Forms of Verbs

On your own paper, rewrite the following sentences. Correct verbs that are in the wrong tense or that use an awkward voice. If a sentence is correct, write *C.*

EX. 1. My friend Vernon, an Ojibwe, has several poems written by him.
My friend Vernon, an Ojibwe, wrote several poems.

1. Another name for the Ojibwe, a large group of American Indians living north of Mexico, will be the Chippewa.
2. Vernon says that the name *Chippewa* was given to them by the U.S. government but that the name *Ojibwe* is preferred by his people.
3. The word *Ojibwe* is meaning "original people" or "spontaneous people."
4. Many Ojibwe now live in an area surrounding the Great Lakes.
5. From Vernon, I learned that the Ojibwe have felt a strong relationship with nature, even if they are now living in a city or town.
6. Before the arrival of Europeans, the Ojibwe believed in taking from nature only what they need for food, clothing, and shelter.
7. The Ojibwe will lose many of their traditions and beliefs when they were put on reservations and sent away to schools run by missionaries.
8. Now, Vernon tells me, the Ojibwe are trying to preserve their culture, and he will have been writing down stories he hears from elders in his tribe.
9. Powwows are held by the Ojibwe, and at these powwows, people join in ceremonial dancing, singing, games, and feasts.
10. Storytelling will also be an important Ojibwe tradition, and this tradition is being carried on by Vernon.

B. Proofreading a Paragraph for the Correct Forms of Verbs

Read the following paragraph. If a sentence contains an error in verb form, draw a line through the incorrect form and write the correct form on the line before the sentence. If the sentence is correct, write *C.*

EX. [1] ____*came*____ My family ~~come~~ to the United States from Greece when I was two years old.

[1] __________ I want to learn as much as I could about Greece. [2] __________ I knew it has a famous history. [3] __________ About 2,500 years ago is a time called the Golden Age of Greece. [4] __________ Plays that were wrote then are still performed today. [5] __________ The style of buildings that were builded then has been copied for many centuries. [6] __________ I also had read stories about the ancient Greek gods and goddesses. [7] __________ My favorite stories are about Artemis, the goddess of the moon. [8] __________ Someday I hope I will have gone to Greece. [9] __________ I regularly write to my cousins who still lived in Greece. [10] __________ They are telling me that they will be very happy if I can come visit them.

C. Using Verbs to Express Time Relationships

The time line below shows several key events from world history. On your own paper, write ten sentences that show time relationships between two or more of the events named. In your sentences, use at least three different tenses.

EX. 1. *The French Revolution began after the Revolutionary War in the United States had started.*

1707 Moguls rule India.

1728 Vitus Bering discovers a passage between America and Asia.

1750 Industrial Revolution begins in Britain.

1775 American Revolutionary War

1789 French Revolution begins.

1815 Napoleon is defeated at Waterloo.

1851 David Livingston explores Africa.

1857 Indians mutiny against British presence in India.

1861 American Civil War begins.

1861 Russia abolishes serfdom.

1909 Robert Peary and Matthew Henderson reach the North Pole.

1911 Amundsen and Scott reach the South Pole.

1914–1918 World War I

1914 Panama Canal Opens.

1936 Spanish Civil War

1939–1945 World War II

1947 Gandhi leads India to independence from Britain.

1700 1800 1900

MODULE 8: USING MODIFIERS CORRECTLY

COMPARISON OF MODIFERS

8a Modifiers change form to show comparison. The three degrees of comparison are *positive, comparative,* and *superlative.*

Positive	Comparative	Superlative
high	higher	highest
tearful	more tearful	most tearful
promptly	more promptly	most promptly

(1) One-syllable modifiers form their comparative and superlative degrees by adding *–er* and *–est.*

Positive	Comparative	Superlative
thick	thicker	thickest
dry	drier	driest

(2) Some two-syllable modifiers form their comparative and superlative degrees by adding *–er* and *–est.* Other two-syllable modifiers form their comparative and superlative degrees with *more* and *most.*

Positive	Comparative	Superlative
lovely	lovelier	loveliest
sticky	stickier	stickiest
awkward	more awkward	most awkward

(3) Modifiers that have more than two syllables form their comparative and superlative degrees with *more* and *most.*

Positive	Comparative	Superlative
generous	more generous	most generous
believably	more believably	most believably

NOTE A few two-syllable modifiers may use either *–er, –est* (*able, abler, ablest*) or *more, most* (*more able, most able*).

(4) Modifiers indicate less or least of a quality with the words *less* and *least.*

Positive	Comparative	Superlative
frequent	less frequent	least frequent
painfully	less painfully	least painfully

NOTE Some modifiers do not follow the regular methods of forming the comparative and superlative degrees.

Positive	Comparative	Superlative
bad	worse	worst
good	better	best
well	better	best
many	more	most

EXERCISE 1 Forming the Degrees of Comparison of Modifiers

On your own paper, write the forms for the comparative and superlative degrees of the modifiers below. Write the comparative and superlative degrees with *less* and *least*, too.

EX. 1. original *more original; less original* *most original; least original*
2. fast *faster; less fast* *fastest; least fast*

1. fragile
2. quiet
3. comfortable
4. friendly
5. silly
6. exciting
7. loudly
8. humid
9. wisely
10. happily
11. courageous
12. lively
13. brief
14. crunchy
15. proud

EXERCISE 2 Using Comparison Forms

On your own paper, write five sentences comparing the items in each of the following pairs. Use the comparative forms of modifiers in your sentences.

EX. 1. china dishes and paper plates
1. *China dishes are stronger than paper plates.*

1. spring and fall
2. books and movies
3. personal computers and typewriters
4. basketball and baseball
5. pens and pencils

MODULE 8: USING MODIFIERS CORRECTLY

USES OF COMPARATIVE AND SUPERLATIVE FORMS

8b Use the comparative degree when comparing two things. Use the superlative degree when comparing more than two.

COMPARATIVE This sweater is **heavier** than that one.
Of the two cats, Muffin was the **more active.**
This month is **less rainy** than last month was.

SUPERLATIVE This sweater is the **heaviest** of all.
Of the three cats, Muffin was the **most active.**
This month was the **least rainy** I can remember.

NOTE In everyday conversation, people sometimes use the superlative degree when comparing two things: *Put your best foot forward.* In writing, however, you should always use the comparative degree when comparing two things.

8c Include the word *other* or *else* when comparing one thing with others in the same group.

NONSTANDARD Hector can draw better than anyone in art class. [As a member of the art class, Hector cannot draw better than himself.]

STANDARD Hector can draw better than anyone **else** in art class.

8d Avoid double comparisons. A double comparison is incorrect because it contains both *–er* and *more* or *–est* and *most.*

NONSTANDARD The second exercise was more harder than the first one.
STANDARD The second exercise was **harder** than the first one.

NONSTANDARD Which bird has the most smallest beak?
STANDARD Which bird has the **smallest** beak?

8e Be sure your comparisons are clear.

UNCLEAR Tamara would rather read books than television.
CLEAR Tamara would rather read books than **watch** television.

EXERCISE 3 Revising Sentences by Correcting Modifiers

Draw a line through the incorrect modifier in each of the following sentences. Write the correct comparative or superlative form above the sentence. Some sentences may be correct.

finer

EX. 1. Some people consider trust a ~~more fine~~ quality than loyalty.

1. Of my two closest friends, Carlos is the most trustworthy.
2. Isaac is the most smartest person I know.
3. My friend Saki is funnier than Clement.
4. I think Emilie has the prettier name of anyone in my class.
5. Which of the two baseball leagues do you like best?
6. W. E. B. Du Bois was one of the more important leaders of the civil rights movement in the United States.
7. Amelia Earhart's flight from Hawaii to California was longer than her flight from the United States to Europe.
8. Of all the artist's paintings, the one in Washington, D.C., is the more widely known.
9. The damage from this year's flood was worser than the damage from last year's drought.
10. Skipper is the gentlest dog I've ever known.
11. Regarding wool and flannel, which is warmest?
12. My grandmother's later quilts are lesser detailed than her earlier ones.
13. In China, the most important visual art is calligraphy.
14. Of the two pairs of scissors, this one is the most sharpest.
15. Ben's speech about Chief Joseph was the more powerful of all the speeches in the class.
16. The Library of Congress is the largest library in the world.
17. Centuries ago, the spice cinnamon was valuabler than gold.
18. Janell thinks couscous is more tastier than oatmeal.
19. The kitchen is the brighter of all the rooms.
20. The sky is more cloudier today than it was yesterday.

MODULE 8: USING MODIFIERS CORRECTLY

DANGLING MODIFIERS

8f A modifying phrase or clause that does not clearly and sensibly modify a word in the same sentence is a *dangling modifier.*

NOTE When a sentence begins with a verbal phrase, the phrase is followed by a comma. The word that the phrase modifies should come immediately after that comma. To correct a dangling modifier, rearrange the words in the sentence, and add or change words to make the meaning logical and clear.

UNCLEAR Weeding the garden, a cabbageworm crawled across my arm.
CLEAR Weeding the garden, **I** felt a cabbageworm crawl across my arm.

NOTE A sentence may appear to have a dangling modifier when *you* is the understood subject. In such cases, the modifier is not dangling; it is modifying the understood subject.

EXAMPLE To take a photograph, (**you**) first focus the lens.

EXERCISE 4 Revising Sentences by Eliminating Dangling Modifiers

On your own paper, revise each of the following sentences to eliminate the dangling modifier. You will have to supply some words to complete the sentences properly.

EX. 1. While standing on the beach, the bay looked misty and cold.
1. *While we were standing on the beach, the bay looked misty and cold.*

1. During yesterday's trail hike, deer grazed in an open field.
2. While resting from our hike, the flock of sea gulls was a soothing sight.
3. Having never lived in the country, seeing deer was a surprise.
4. Watching the deer, a marvelous feeling came over me.
5. To become a naturalist, natural history should be studied.
6. After hiking back to camp, a crisp apple was refreshing.
7. Preparing the campfire and then cooking and eating dinner, the evening passed quietly.
8. To see the stars at their brightest, we suggest getting away from city lights.
9. After waking up in the chilly morning air, a breakfast of steaming oatmeal is warming.
10. To cross the bay, the ferry at the peninsula dock should be taken.

EXERCISE 5 Writing Sentences with Introductory Modifiers

On the lines below, write complete sentences using the introductory modifiers given. Be sure that the word modified by the introduction immediately follows the comma.

EX. 1. To understand the experiment,

To understand the experiment, Kathleen reviewed her chemistry module.

1. To prepare for class, ______________________

____

2. To make sure she wouldn't oversleep, ______________________

____

3. Having arrived early, ______________________

____

4. Quietly voicing his opinion, ______________________

____

5. Setting the table, ______________________

____

6. Hopping from leaf to leaf, ______________________

____

7. While making his breakfast, ______________________

____

8. To avoid the crowd, ______________________

____

9. Writing her first term paper, ______________________

____

10. Performing before the large audience, ______________________

____

MODULE 8: USING MODIFIERS CORRECTLY

MISPLACED MODIFIERS

8g A modifying phrase or clause that makes a sentence awkward or unclear because it seems to modify the wrong word or group of words is a *misplaced modifier*.

Modifying phrases should be placed as near as possible to the words they modify.

MISPLACED Mr. Ogata noticed rotting wood painting his house trim.
CORRECTED **Painting his house trim,** Mr. Ogata noticed rotting wood.

8h Adjective clauses and adverb clauses should be placed where they are clearly linked to the words they modify.

To correct a misplaced clause, place the modifying clause as close as possible to the word or words that it modifies.

MISPLACED The tennis racket is still in my car that I meant to return to you.
CORRECTED The tennis racket **that I meant to return to you** is still in my car.

EXERCISE 6 Revising Sentences by Correcting Misplaced Modifiers

Revise each of the following sentences by moving the misplaced phrase or clause near the word or words it modifies.

EX. 1. Felicia saw the shooting stars in the sky with her brother.
With her brother, Felicia saw the shooting stars in the sky.

1. Mr. Fitzgerald entertained us with stories about sea monsters in his living room. ______________________________

____

2. Jorge poured the milk for the kitten in a bowl. ______________________________

____

3. Turning cartwheels, the audience applauded as Vanessa left the stage.

____

____

4. Mateo and Betsy could see the ants climbing the hill with their magnifying glasses.

5. Blue and yellow, Alex was amazed by the colors of the butterfly.

6. A board game was discovered by an archaeologist, thought to be the oldest in the world.

7. There are several people in our office waiting for the doctor, which has just been repainted.

8. An old piece of cheddar cheese sat in the refrigerator that was covered with mold.

9. Frank crossed the street on his bicycle, which was busy with rush-hour traffic.

10. A tenth-century Chinese cook invented fireworks in his kitchen that exploded with sparks.

11. He ate a pear and two apples baby-sitting Tony and Jessica.

12. My sister and I could see the dark funnel cloud approaching from the bedroom window.

13. I gave a dozen cucumbers to my next-door neighbor that I had picked from the garden.

14. Jacqueline showed the rocking chair to her friends that she had refinished.

15. As a child, my mother taught me how to swim.

MODULE 8: USING MODIFIERS CORRECTLY

MODULE REVIEW

A. Revising Sentences by Correcting Modifiers

In each sentence below, underline any error in the use of modifiers. Write the correct form in the space above the sentence.

more difficult

EX. 1. Finding the brightest star in tonight's sky was ~~difficulter~~ than finding it in last night's sky.

1. Which constellation do you see most often, Leo Minor or Pegasus?
2. Since the most earliest times, groups of stars have been named after mythical characters and objects.
3. Astronomers found it least difficult to identify groups of stars rather than individual ones.
4. The ancient astronomer Ptolemy is more interesting to me than any astronomer.
5. With fewer exceptions, the names of the constellations in Ptolemy's catalog are still used today.
6. Ptolemy believed that of all the planets, Earth was nearer to the center of the universe.
7. The most brightest "stars" in the sky are not true stars at all, but planets.
8. The planet most close to the sun is Mercury.
9. The most smallest and most distant planet, Pluto was not discovered until 1930.
10. To me the dry Martian riverbeds are more interesting than any planetary feature.

B. Writing Sentences Using the Comparative and Superlative Forms of Modifiers

At the beginning of the twentieth century, teenagers thought a ride on an elaborate, hand-carved carousel was exciting. Today, as we approach the year 2000, young people are more likely to be interested in a wild roller-coaster ride! Picture a carousel of horses painted in fanciful colors, ridden by women in large hats and long skirts and by men wearing top hats. Now, picture a roller coaster, cars filled with screaming teenagers. Write five sentences using comparative forms of adverbs and adjectives to compare the two rides. Then write five sentences comparing three rides—the carousel, the roller coaster, and a ride you imagine will be a favorite at the turn of the twenty-second century.

After you use at least two modifiers from each box, you may use any other modifiers that you wish.

bright	happy	good	intense	exciting
simple	high	many	colorful	stressful
young	pretty	little	expensive	thrilling
scary	fast	much	compelling	mature
safe	long	bad	enjoyable	romantic

EX. 1. *The carousel is more romantic but less thrilling than the roller coaster.*

C. Using Modifiers Correctly in a Paragraph

On your own paper, correct the misplaced or incorrect modifiers in the paragraph below.

EX. [1] Two students enjoy bird-watching in our class.

1. *Two students in our class enjoy bird-watching.*

[1] Pedro has a better knowledge of birds than anyone I know. [2] However, Leah thinks her sister Sara knows more about grosbeaks and finches than Pedro. [3] Sara said that the grosbeak's song is softer than the purple finch. [4] Smaller than the grosbeak, Pedro once saw a white-winged crossbill. [5] Pedro and Sara agree that the grosbeak is the larger of all northern finches. [6] Known for their well-hidden nests, Sara has patiently watched for winter wrens. [7] Sara explained how the winter wren moves like a mouse in a class presentation. [8] More shyer than the song sparrow, Pedro told us about the features of the Lincoln's sparrow in his presentation. [9] Walking in a bog, the shy sparrow sings its rich, bubbling song. [10] After completing their presentations, the applause lasted until the class bell rang.

MODULE 9: A GLOSSARY OF USAGE

ACCEPT, EXCEPT / AT

This module contains an alphabetical list of common problems in English usage. Throughout the module, examples are labeled *standard* or *nonstandard*. ***Standard English*** is the most widely accepted form of English. ***Nonstandard English*** is language that does not follow the rules and guidelines of standard English.

accept, except *Accept* is a verb that means "to receive." *Except* may be either a verb or a preposition. As a verb, *except* means "to leave out" or "to exclude"; as a preposition, *except* means "other than" or "excluding."

EXAMPLES Please **accept** this award.
Please do not **except** Peter from the team. [verb]
I practice piano every day **except** Saturday. [preposition]

affect, effect *Affect* is a verb meaning "to influence." *Effect* used as a verb means "to bring about." Used as a noun, *effect* means "the result of some action."

EXAMPLES The heavy flooding **affected** the crops.
The mayor **effected** many changes in the government. [verb]
The scarecrow had no **effect** on the birds. [noun]

all the farther, all the faster These expressions are used informally in some parts of the country to mean "as far as" and "as fast as."

NONSTANDARD This is all the farther we can go.
STANDARD This is **as far as** we can go.

allusion, illusion An *allusion* is a reference to something. An *illusion* is a mistaken idea or a misleading appearance.

EXAMPLES Her speech made an **allusion** to the stories of Edgar Allan Poe.
The documentary shattered **illusions** about the war.
The magician was a master of **illusion.**

among, between Use *among* when referring to all members of a group rather than to separate individuals in the group. Use *between* when you are referring to two things at a time, even if they are part of a larger group.

EXAMPLES We distributed the toys **among** the children.
There is a strong bond **between** England and the United States.

and etc. *Etc.* is an abbreviation of the Latin *et cetera,* which means "and other things." Thus, *etc.* includes *and.*

EXAMPLE I earn money by baby-sitting, mowing lawns, **etc.** [not *and etc.*]

anywheres, everywheres, nowheres, somewheres Use these words without the *s* at the end.

EXAMPLE **Anywhere** you travel, you can find the same hotel chains.

as See **like, as.**

at Do not use *at* after *where.*

EXAMPLE Where did you see them? [not *see them at*]

EXERCISE 1 Identifying Correct Usage

For each sentence below, underline the correct word in parentheses.

EX. 1. Her sister lives (*somewheres, somewhere*) in Europe.

1. The audience was deeply (*affected, effected*) by her piano solo.
2. You can choose from (*among, between*) many national parks in the United States for a camping vacation.
3. The full moon was so bright that it gave the (*allusion, illusion*) of daylight.
4. Did everyone (*accept, except*) Julian arrive on time?
5. Some people believe that painting a room blue gives it a soothing (*affect, effect*).

EXERCISE 2 Proofreading a Paragraph to Correct Errors in Usage

In each sentence in the paragraph below, draw a line through the error in usage. Then write the correct usage in the space above the word. Some sentences may contain no errors.

accept

EX. [1] The artist stood up to ~~except~~ the award.

[1] He spoke about the many years he had spent traveling anywheres he could to find subjects for his paintings. [2] He lived in Tanzania, between villagers in the Masai country. [3] The audience laughed when he described how he tried to climb Mount Kilimanjaro: The base of the mountain was all the farther he could get. [4] He also painted the wildlife and the countryside, and etc. [5] His talk was short, but it had a powerful affect on the people listening; everyone was eager to see his award-winning paintings and drawings.

MODULE 9: A GLOSSARY OF USAGE

BEING AS, BEING THAT / INVENT, DISCOVER

being as, being that Avoid using these expressions. Use *because* or *since* instead.

NONSTANDARD Being as her grades were so high, she got a scholarship.
STANDARD **Because** her grades were so high, she got a scholarship.
NONSTANDARD Being that he was late, he missed the beginning of the play.
STANDARD **Since** he was late, he missed the beginning of the play.

between, among See **among.**

bust, busted Avoid using these words as verbs. Use a form of *break* or *burst* instead.

EXAMPLE **I broke** the chain on my bicycle. [not *busted*]

could of Do not use *of* with the helping verb *could.* Use *could have* instead. Also avoid *had of, ought to of, should of, would of, might of,* and *must of.*

EXAMPLE Sam **could have** gone with us. [not *could of*]

discover, invent *Discover* means "to find, see, or learn about something that already exists." *Invent* means "to be the first to make or do something."

EXAMPLES William Herschel **discovered** the planet Uranus.
The game of checkers was **invented** in ancient Egypt.

effect See **affect, effect.**

See **anywheres,** etc.

fewer, less *Fewer* is used with plural nouns. It tells "how many." *Less* is used with singular nouns. It tells "how much."

EXAMPLES We saw **fewer** whales this summer.
This fruit punch contains **less** sugar than that one does.

good, well *Good* is an adjective. Do not use it to modify a verb. Use *well* instead.

NONSTANDARD She skis good.
STANDARD She skis **well.**

had of See **could of.**

illusion See **allusion, illusion.**

invent, discover See **discover.**

EXERCISE 3 Identifying Correct Usage

For each sentence below, underline the correct word in parentheses.

EX. 1. We (*should of, should have*) turned off the lights.

1. The game *Parcheesi* was (*discovered, invented*) in India.
2. The (*affect, effect*) of the food was to make them ill.
3. We saw (*fewer, less*) hawks this year on our bird-watching trip.
4. Tranh plays the piano (*good, well*).
5. Do you know who (*invented, discovered*) the cave?
6. Jason (*broke, busted*) the lamp during the experiment.
7. I wish I (*could of, could have*) gone to the concert.
8. Anders thought the play was very (*good, well*) done.
9. Her test scores were (*good, well*).
10. The next time I make bread I will use (*fewer, less*) yeast.

EXERCISE 4 Proofreading a Paragraph to Correct Errors in Usage

In the paragraph below, draw a line through each error in usage. Then write the correct usage in the space above each word. Some sentences may contain no errors.

fewer
EX. [1] Scott owns no ~~less~~ than three umbrellas.

[1] The umbrella originated in Mesopotamia around 1400 B.C. [2] The reason that the umbrella was discovered was not to keep out rain. [3] Instead, the early umbrella was a protection from the affects of the sun. [4] Along with fans, people used umbrellas everywheres to keep cool. [5] Before this invention, no one would of thought anything could work as good as the fan. [6] Later in Egypt, the umbrella had religious meaning. [7] Being as Egyptians believed that there was a goddess of the heavens, they thought the umbrella represented her. [8] Therefore, only kings and queens could have umbrellas held over their heads. [9] It was considered a special privilege between royal families to stand under an umbrella. [10] These customs endured good for many centuries.

MODULE 9: A GLOSSARY OF USAGE

KIND, SORT, TYPE / SHOULD OF

kind, sort, type These words should always agree in number with the words *this* and *that* (singular) or *these* and *those* (plural).

EXAMPLE Those **kinds** of flowers grow wild; however, this **type** is a garden flower.

kind of a, sort of a The *a* (or *an)* is unnecessary. Omit it.

EXAMPLE This motor needs a special **kind of** filter [not *kind of a*]

learn, teach *Learn* means "to acquire information." *Teach* means "to instruct" or "to show."

EXAMPLES Maya **taught** me Spanish.
She **learned** to speak Spanish in Mexico.

let, leave *Leave* means "to go away." *Let* means "to allow or permit."

NONSTANDARD Leave them go.
STANDARD **Let** them go.

less, fewer See **fewer, less.**

like, as, as if *Like* is usually a preposition. In informal English, *like* is often used in place of the conjunctions *as, as if,* or *as though.* Formal English calls for one of these conjunctions to introduce a subordinate clause.

EXAMPLES The shadow looked **like** a shark in the water. [*Like* introduces the prepositional phrase *like a shark.*]
It had a fin **as** a shark does. [The conjunction *as* introduces the subordinate clause.]
It looked **as if** (or **as though**) it might swim by us.

nowheres See **anywheres.**

of Do not use *of* with prepositions such as *inside, off,* and *outside.*

EXAMPLES The diver jumped **off** the diving board. [not *off of*]
Outside the restaurant was a garden. [not *outside of*]

off of See **of.**

ought to of See **could of.**

should of See **could of.**

EXERCISE 5 Identifying Correct Usage

For each sentence below, underline the correct word or words in parentheses.

EX. 1. Please (<u>*let*</u>, *leave*) the dog stay in the house.

1. It looked (*like, as*) a spider on the wall.
2. Out of (*nowhere, nowheres*) came a baseball.
3. I'm looking for a certain (*kind of, kind of a*) button.
4. (*Let, Leave*) Carlos tell about the Mayans.
5. We sold (*fewer, less*) tickets than we expected.
6. Does it shed its skin (*like, as*) a lizard does?
7. Tanya frightened the bird (*off, off of*) the rock.
8. His grandmother tried to (*learn, teach*) us how to sing the song.
9. Yusef (*ought to, ought to of*) enter his photographs in the contest.
10. Andreas usually wins (*this, these*) type of game.

EXERCISE 6 Proofreading a Paragraph to Correct Errors in Usage

In the paragraph below, draw a line through each error in usage. Then write the correct usage in the space above the word. Some sentences may contain no errors.

EX. [1] The small ball of fur meowed ~~like~~ *as* a kitten does.

[1] I ought to of known better, but I never can resist kittens. [2] This kitten seemed to have come out of nowheres. [3] I found it sitting just outside the fence. [4] It looked like a tiny kind of a tiger. [5] It looked hungry and cold, too. [6] Since a blizzard was coming, I let the cat come inside of my house. [7] I thought it would be all right to leave the cat stay for a night. [8] It found the most comfortable place in the house, like a cat always does. [9] I moved it a few times off of the chair by the fireplace before I gave up and let it sleep there. [10] I guess we will get along pretty well—if only I can learn it to share my favorite chair with me.

MODULE 9: A GLOSSARY OF USAGE

SOME, SOMEWHAT / WOULD OF

some, somewhat Do not use *some* as an adverb in place of *somewhat.*

EXAMPLE This medicine should help your allergy **somewhat.** [not *some*]

sort See **kind, sort, type.**

sort of See **kind of, sort of.**

teach See **learn, teach.**

than, then *Than* is a conjunction used in comparisons. *Then* is an adverb telling "when."

EXAMPLES He is shorter **than** I.
I did my homework; **then** I went for a run.

them Do not use *them* as an adjective. Use *those* instead.

EXAMPLE It's one of **those** surprise endings. [not *them*]

this here, this there *Here* and *there* are unnecessary after *this* and *that.*

EXAMPLE Let's try **this** trail. [not *this here*]

try and The correct expression is *try to.*

EXAMPLE When you play this game, **try to** concentrate. [not *try and*]

type See **kind, sort, type.**

way, ways Use *way*, not *ways*, in referring to a distance.

EXAMPLE The school is quite a **way** from here. [not *ways*]

well See **good, well.**

what Do not use *what* in place of *that* to introduce a subordinate clause.

EXAMPLE This is the article **that** I told you about. [not *what*]

when, where Do not use *when* or *where* incorrectly in writing a definition.

NONSTANDARD A debate is where people present different opinions about issues.
STANDARD A debate is a presentation of differing viewpoints.

where Do not use *where* for *that.*

EXAMPLE I read **that** Constitution Day is a holiday in Thailand. [not *where*]

which, that, who *Which* refers only to things. *That* refers to either people or things. *Who* refers only to people.

EXAMPLES The Louvre Museum, **which** is quite famous, is in Paris.

This is the part **that** I need for the engine.

Is she the one **that** you are waiting for?

He is the one **who** called earlier.

would of See **could of.**

EXERCISE 7 Correcting Errors in Usage

In the sentences below, draw a line through each error in usage. Then write the correct usage in the space above the word.

those

EX. 1. This book is one of ~~them~~ bestsellers.

1. This here book is really funny.
2. My brother is younger then I am.
3. A dispute is when two people can't agree.
4. The quarterback threw quite a long ways for a touchdown.
5. A tornado is where you have a violent, whirling wind accompanied by a funnel-shaped cloud.
6. Ruth is the one which won the race.
7. I am going to try and find a job.
8. This lotion relieves the itch of poison ivy some.
9. It's one of them dress-up parties.
10. I read where there is a celebration in Mexico called *La Fiesta de las Posadas*.
11. First the strawberries become ripe, than the raspberries.
12. In sailing, a regatta is where several boats meet to race.
13. Dena likes basketball better then baseball.
14. We decided to try this here beach for a change.
15. Where did you find them flowers?

MODULE 9: A GLOSSARY OF USAGE

THE DOUBLE NEGATIVE

A ***double negative*** is the use of two negative words when one is enough.

NONSTANDARD She did not have no time to finish her work.
STANDARD She **did not have time** to finish her work.

hardly, scarcely Do not use the words *hardly* or *scarcely* with another negative word.

NONSTANDARD There are scarcely no more blue whales left in the ocean.
STANDARD There are **scarcely** any blue whales left in the ocean.

no, none, nothing Do not use any of these negative words with another negative word.

NONSTANDARD There isn't no reason to be worried.
STANDARD There **is no** reason to be worried.
NONSTANDARD I didn't hear nothing.
STANDARD I **didn't hear anything.** or I **heard nothing.**

EXERCISE 8 Correcting Errors in Usage

In each of the following sentences, underline the error in usage. Write the correct form above the error.

anything
EX. 1. I've never seen <u>nothing</u> as beautiful as Yosemite National Park.

1. It was so foggy you couldn't hardly see the road.
2. Elena didn't have no pictures of her hometown in Costa Rica.
3. Don't you cook no vegetables?
4. We didn't have no more time.
5. They hadn't hardly started walking when Joshua said his feet hurt.
6. I didn't have nothing to read while I waited for the train to arrive.
7. Lee asked for a map of the Navajo reservation, but they didn't have none.
8. There weren't no seats left for the concert.
9. We hadn't scarcely enough room for all the people who came to see the dancers from the South Pacific.
10. After her gerbil got loose in the house, Sofia said she didn't want no more pets.
11. I hadn't seen no eclipse before!

12. Wyatt looked for the missing socks but didn't find none.
13. Cecilia hadn't never been to the Chinese New Year's parade.
14. Before we went to visit her, our neighbor hadn't never told anyone about her homeland, which is Vietnam.
15. Didn't you hear nothing?
16. There isn't no easy way to the top of Mount Everest.
17. He doesn't know nothing about fixing cars.
18. Mimi couldn't hardly go to the city all alone.
19. Before I went to Mexico, I hadn't never tasted spicy foods.
20. I heard a sound outside, but I didn't see nothing.

EXERCISE 9 Using Negatives Correctly in Sentences

You are the Safety Officer on Space Station IV. You have been asked to create a list of safety tips to give to all new workers coming from Earth. On your own paper, create ten safety tips. Write each safety tip as a sentence, using a negative in at least five of your tips.

EX. 1. *Do not enter the space lock without your spacesuit.*

MODULE 9: A GLOSSARY OF USAGE

MODULE REVIEW

A. Correcting Errors in Usage

In each sentence below, draw a line through the error in usage. Then write the correct usage in the space above the word. Some sentences may contain no errors.

any

EX. 1. We didn't get ~~no~~ rain this summer.

1. The Iroquois discovered the game of lacrosse.
2. There are scarcely no more wolves left in the United States, except for in Alaska.
3. Why are these sorts of games really complicated to play?
4. Place a mirror on that wall to give the allusion of a bigger room.
5. We saw fewer wildflowers this year then last year.
6. This low-cholesterol recipe calls for less egg yolks.
7. Have you ever read this here book called *Of Mice and Men*?
8. I knew I'd left my homework somewheres.
9. Marie and Pierre Curie invented radium.
10. We searched for clues but didn't find nothing.
11. Reindeer and others of these hardy type of animal live in the Arctic.
12. Did you hear where the town wants to build a public swimming pool?
13. It was hard to choose between all of the fine entries in the science contest.
14. Shirley Chisholm was the first African American woman which was elected to Congress.
15. Jordan said he would let us go to the museum.
16. Her powerful speech about the rights of working people really effected the audience.
17. Vanda's story made an allusion to Tokyo's Kabuki Theater.
18. The Tour de France is a bicycle race that goes quite a long ways around France.
19. We were lucky we didn't have no hurricanes this year.
20. I must of left my books on the bus.

B. Correcting Errors in Usage

In the paragraph below, underline the errors in usage. Then write the correct usage in the space above the word. Some sentences contain no errors.

except

EX. [1] All of these tribes accept the Cherokee belonged to the Iroquois Confederacy.

[1] Being as the five nations of the Iroquois were tired of fighting, they formed a peace pact between the tribes. [2] They called themselves the *Ongwanonhsioni*, which means "people of the long house," because their lands lay next to each other just as the long houses they built. [3] They held council meetings that were attended by leaders from everywheres in the Iroquois territory. [4] Nothing could never be decided at these councils unless all fifty leaders, or sachems, agreed.

[5] To keep records of these meetings, the Iroquois used wampum. [6] Wampum was where they arranged beads in meaningful patterns. [7] The beads, who were made of seashells, were strung together and sewn into leather belts. [8] At the end of the council meetings, wampum was exchanged. [9] If the leaders didn't agree, sometimes they didn't exchange no wampum. [10] Today people try and read the wampum belts; but the belts are so old, no one living knows their meaning.

C. Writing a Newspaper Article

You are a reporter who has been assigned to write an article for the "Lifestyle" section of your newspaper. The article is about a special celebration that takes place in your community. In at least ten sentences, describe this event, and discuss its origins or its meaning to the community. In this article, use at least five of the expressions that are covered in this module. Underline these expressions. Double-check to make sure you are using the correct form.

EX. *Let me tell you about the street fair in our town. This fair, which raises money for a local church, is held in the middle of the summer.*

MODULE 10: CAPITAL LETTERS

PEOPLE AND PLACES

10a Capitalize the names of persons.

EXAMPLES **I**gor **S**travinsky, **A**lice **W**alker, **M**s. **N**icole **A**rzola

The abbreviations *Jr.* (*junior*) and *Sr.* (*senior*) should always be capitalized.

EXAMPLES **J**erome **W**. **W**ilson, **J**r. **S**imon **L**. **S**nyder, **S**r.

10b Capitalize geographical names.

Type of Name	Examples
towns, cities	**H**ouston, **A**lbany, **J**ackson, **B**ridgeport
counties, states	**O**cean **C**ounty, **P**enobscot **C**ounty, **U**tah
countries	**I**ndia, **C**roatia, **B**elize, **J**apan, **K**enya
islands	**N**antucket, **S**icily, **P**uerto **R**ico, **S**ri **L**anka
bodies of water	**A**mazon **R**iver, **B**oston **H**arbor, **G**ulf of **M**exico
forests, parks	**S**herwood **F**orest, **S**henandoah **N**ational **P**ark
streets, highways	**J**ewett **S**treet, **M**assachusetts **T**urnpike, **R**oute 81
mountains	**M**ount **E**verest, **A**ppalachian **M**ountains
continents	**A**frica, **N**orth **A**merica, **A**ustralia, **A**sia
regions	the **M**idwest, **L**ake **R**egion, the **N**orth

NOTE Words such as *east, west, north,* and *south* are not capitalized when they indicate direction.

EXAMPLES We drove south on the parkway.
Sula's town is east of my town.

NOTE In a hyphenated street number, the second part of the number is not capitalized.

EXAMPLE West Sixty-eighth Street

EXERCISE 1 Correcting Errors in Capitalization

For the sentences below, correct the errors in capitalization by drawing a line through each incorrect letter and writing the correct form above it.

E A

EX. 1. We will be traveling west on ~~e~~ssex ~~a~~venue.

1. With my friend alma, I watched the sun rise from cadillac mountain.
2. My favorite writer, maya angelou, lived in stamps, arkansas.
3. Reeds have been used to make roofs on structures in africa and north america.
4. Did you know that henry david thoreau lived by walden pond in concord, massachusetts?
5. We traveled South on route 95 and then took washington street to get to brooklyn botanic garden.
6. My school is located on west seventy-eighth street in apple ridge county.
7. The lowest point in the united states is death valley.
8. Our friends, the chens, visited king's canyon national park.
9. The country of vietnam is located in southeast asia.
10. My teacher, mr. bill james, sr., has lived in the south all his life.

EXERCISE 2 Proofreading Sentences for Correct Capitalization

In the sentences below, underline the words that should be capitalized. Write the correct form in the space above the word. Some sentences may be correct.

Caribbean Sea *Cancún*

EX. 1. We swam in the caribbean sea on a trip to cancún.

1. My friend jane won a scuba-diving trip to the florida keys.
2. Dale is moving to helena, which is the capital of montana.
3. I stayed with my aunt, irisa Mendoza, in san juan, puerto rico.
4. States in the Northeast experienced cooler temperatures last night.
5. Our house in essex county is right off the garden state parkway.

MODULE 10: CAPITAL LETTERS

SCHOOL SUBJECTS, FIRST WORDS, PROPER ADJECTIVES

10c Capitalize the first word in every sentence.

EXAMPLES The red panda eats plants. **It** is related to the raccoon.

The first word of a sentence that is a direct quotation is capitalized even if the quotation begins within a sentence.

EXAMPLE Shelby answered, "**We** were just rehearsing with our band."

Traditionally, the first word in a line of poetry is capitalized.

EXAMPLES **Wind** was rough that winter night.
It tossed the boats with all its might,
But we stayed warm by the firelight.

The pronoun *I* and the interjection *O* are capitalized whether or not they are the first words of a sentence. The common interjection *oh* is capitalized only when it begins a sentence or is part of a title.

EXAMPLES Sam and **I** won the race, and, **oh**, was **I** tired.
The story began, "Help me, **O** Great One, for **I** am lost."

10d Capitalize proper nouns and proper adjectives.

A ***proper adjective*** is formed from a proper noun.

Proper Nouns	Proper Adjectives
Mexico	Mexican blanket
Louis Braille	Braille alphabet
Shakespeare	Shakespearean drama

NOTE Proper nouns and adjectives may lose their capitals through frequent use.

EXAMPLES bologna pasteurized diesel

10e Do *not* capitalize the names of school subjects, except for names of languages and course names followed by a number.

EXAMPLE This semester, Chantel is taking **E**nglish, **L**atin, **e**arth **s**cience, **a**rt, and **G**eometry II.

EXERCISE 3 Using Capital Letters Correctly

For the sentences below, correct the errors in capitalization by drawing a line through each incorrect letter and writing the correct form above it.

EX. 1. ~~w~~e walked to the corner market and bought bread. (W)

1. I'm taking a spanish class this year.
2. My sister said, "read my essay, please."
3. Karuna's favorite subjects are Algebra and German.
4. Anne wrote, "if we cannot attend, i will call you."
5. My cousin has a recipe for irish soda bread.
6. Give Misha a copy of our latin vocabulary list.
7. Have you ever tried brazil nuts?
8. my favorite poet of the Harlem renaissance is Countee Cullen.
9. We worked with a Bunsen burner today in our Science class.
10. "please tell Angelo about my birthday party," Luna said.
11. The parade began in the morning. we saw some beautiful floats.
12. The best line in Azi's poem is "oh, the moon was a glowing pearl."
13. My grandmother told us about lithuanian traditions.
14. The principal walked onstage and said, "welcome, everyone."
15. Our apartment is in a beautiful victorian house.
16. She said, "guide me, o wondrous stars."
17. I want to learn more about dolphins because i find them interesting.
18. that beautiful branched candleholder is a menorah.
19. A poem started, "puppies with floppy ears and sloppy tongues."
20. Clea signed up for chemistry II.
21. Please ask for extra rice when you order the chinese food.
22. Ten burmese musicians will present a concert tonight.
23. All at once, Lainie shouted, "oh, no! the cake is burning!"
24. main Street in our town is lined with old brick buildings and ends at a white-spired church.
25. would you please make me a Bologna sandwich?

MODULE 10: CAPITAL LETTERS

GROUPS, ORGANIZATIONS, AND RELIGIONS

10f Capitalize the names of teams, organizations, businesses, institutions, buildings, and government bodies.

Type of Name	Examples
teams	**C**hicago **W**hite **S**ox, **P**hiladelphia **F**lyers, **L**os **A**ngeles **D**odgers
organizations	**I**nternational **R**ed **C**ross **W**orld **H**ealth **O**rganization
businesses	**J**alapeño's **M**exican **R**estaurant **C**aboose **T**ravel **S**ervice
institutions	**F**lorida **S**tate **U**niversity, **B**oston **L**atin **S**chool, **E**merson **C**ollege
buildings	**A**llen **T**heater, **E**iffel **T**ower
government bodies	**D**epartment of **H**ealth and **H**uman **S**ervices, **U**nited **S**tates **C**ongress

NOTE Do not capitalize words such as *democratic, republican*, and *socialist* when they refer to principles or forms of government. Capitalize these words only when they refer to a specific political party.

EXAMPLES We used a **d**emocratic process to elect club officers.
The **R**epublicans are having their convention.

The word *party* in the name of a political party may or may not be capitalized; either way is correct.

EXAMPLES the **D**emocratic **p**arty (*or* **P**arty)

10g Capitalize the names of specific nationalities and peoples.

EXAMPLES **A**frican **A**merican, **C**aucasian, **A**sian, **H**ispanic, **C**herokee, **K**orean, **R**omanian

10h Capitalize the names of religions and their followers, holy days and celebrations, sacred writings, and specific deities.

EXAMPLES **B**uddhism, **C**hristianity, **T**aoist, **M**ormon, **Y**om **K**ippur, **E**piphany, **N**ew **T**estament, **K**oran, **T**orah, **G**od, **A**llah, **B**uddha

EXERCISE 4 Identifying Correct Capitalization

Write the letter *C* on the line before each phrase that is capitalized correctly.

EX. _____ 1. a. the minnesota twins
_C___ b. the Minnesota Twins

_______ 1. a. the Republican Party
_______ b. the republican party

_______ 2. a. Roxbury Community College
_______ b. roxbury community college

_______ 3. a. Department of Energy
_______ b. department of energy

_______ 4. a. the Humane society
_______ b. the Humane Society

_______ 5. a. the Iroquois
_______ b. the Iroquois

_______ 6. a. International Court of Justice
_______ b. International Court of justice

_______ 7. a. Dragon Light Restaurant
_______ b. dragon light restaurant

_______ 8. a. farm creek construction
_______ b. Farm Creek Construction

_______ 9. a. U.S. Coast Guard
_______ b. U.S. coast guard

_______ 10. a. San Diego padres
_______ b. San Diego Padres

EXERCISE 5 Proofreading Sentences for Correct Capitalization

For each sentence below, correct the errors in capitalization by drawing a line through each incorrect letter and writing the correct form above it.

EX. 1. Do you know many ~~h~~(H)anukkah songs?

1. My canadian relatives visited for easter.
2. My sister works for new england telephone.
3. I gave money to save the children, an international organization.
4. We learned about the muslim fast of ramadan.
5. That store sells items made by haitian artists.

MODULE 10: CAPITAL LETTERS

OBJECTS, EVENTS, AND AWARDS

10i Capitalize the brand names of business products.

EXAMPLES Apple computer, Minute Maid juice, Noxzema skin cream

NOTE The word showing the type of product is not capitalized.

10j Capitalize the names of historical events and periods, special events and holidays, and other calendar items.

EXAMPLES Louisiana Purchase, Harlem Renaissance, Tony Awards, Feast of St. Anthony, Tuesday, Chinese New Year

10k Capitalize the names of ships, monuments, awards, planets, and any other particular places, things, or events.

Type of Name	Examples
ships, trains	USS *Chesapeake*, Burlington *Zephyr*
aircraft, spacecraft, missiles	*Spruce Goose, Apollo I*, Gemini-Titan
monuments, memorials	Lincoln Memorial, Ether Monument
awards	National Merit Scholarship
planets, stars	Jupiter, Polaris

EXERCISE 6 Proofreading Sentences for Correct Capitalization

Each of the following sentences contains errors in capitalization. Write your corrections on the lines provided, and separate your answers with a semicolon. Write *C* if the sentence is correct.

EX. 1. At johnson space center, I saw pictures of the *apollo I* taking off.

Johnson Space Center; Apollo I

1. On a dark night we can see the constellation orion.

____

2. The *Monitor* was an armored ship built during the Civil War.

____

3. Have you been inside the statue of liberty?

____

4. The writer Toni Morrison won the nobel prize in 1993.

___

5. We went to the dentist on the monday just after new year's day.

___

6. It was bastille day, so we learned about French customs.

___

7. The downtown area is a busy place from monday to friday.

___

8. Sheena did a report on the war of 1812.

___

9. In 1666, London, England, experienced a tragic event called the Great Fire.

___

10. The beautiful taj mahal is a famous marble structure in India.

___

11. We bought Dial soap and Comet cleanser for the bathroom.

___

12. Did you read the book about our galaxy, the milky way?

___

13. That wonderful documentary won an emmy award last september.

___

14. The uss *constitution* is open to tourists.

___

15. My father bought a box of gorton's fish for our memorial day picnic.

___

MODULE 10: CAPITAL LETTERS

TITLES

10l Capitalize titles.

(1) Capitalize the title of a person when the title comes before the name.

EXAMPLES The university honored **D**r. Chatterjee last night.
She saw **P**resident Clinton when he toured the country.

(2) Capitalize a word showing family relationship when the word is used before or in place of a person's name, but not when preceded by a possessive pronoun.

EXAMPLES We went to the lake with **D**ad and **A**unt Luisa.
We went to the lake with my **d**ad and my **a**unt Luisa.

(3) Capitalize the first and last words and all important words in titles of books, magazines, newspapers, poems, short stories, historical documents, movies, television programs, works of art, and musical compositions.

Unimportant words in titles include articles (*a, an, the*), coordinating conjunctions (*and, but, for, nor, or, so, yet*), and prepositions of fewer than five letters (*at, for, from, with and so on*).

NOTE The article *the* preceding a title is not capitalized unless it is the first word of the title.

EXAMPLE Devon enjoys reading the *Georgetown Weekly.*

Type of Title	**Examples**
books	*The **R**ed **P**ony, **N**ative **S**on*
newspapers	***D**etroit **F**ree **P**ress, **T**he **N**ew **Y**ork **T**imes*
magazines	***N**ewsweek, **E**bony, **S**eventeen*
poems	*"**T**he **F**ish," "**M**orning **S**ong"*
short stories	"**S**onny's **B**lues," "**E**veryday **U**se"
historical documents	**E**mancipation **P**roclamation
movies	***F**inding **N**emo, **G**uardians of the **G**alaxy*
television programs	***G**ood **L**uck **C**harlie, **A**merican **I**dol*
works of art	***M**oon **R**iver, **M**ona **L**isa*
musical compositions	"**Mambo No. 5**," *The **M**ikado*

EXERCISE 7 Proofreading for Correct Capitalization

For the sentences below, correct the errors in capitalization by drawing a line through each capitalization error and writing the correct form above it.

Senator

EX. 1. Write a letter to ~~senator~~ Kennedy about that issue.

1. I've heard a lot about Ralph Ellison's book, *invisible man.*
2. Cassandra still has that issue of *essence.*
3. Give mom that message from aunt Clarice.
4. I enjoy Langston Hughes's poetry, especially a poem called "dream variations."
5. We all wrote a letter to the editor of the *des moines register.*
6. I know that uncle Pat has learned many new recipes from the TV show *great chefs of the east.*
7. My favorite book used to be E. B. White's *charlotte's web.*
8. We took Shayla to dr. Ron Serrano when she had the flu.
9. My little brother often watches the show *reading rainbow.*
10. The painting style called Impressionism began with Claude Monet's painting *impression: sunrise.*
11. I went with cousin Al to see the declaration of independence.
12. We recently streamed the movie *black panther*, starring Chadwick Boseman.
13. My sister bought grandpa the book *among schoolchildren.*
14. Has professor Goldstein written another book lately?
15. My teacher read us an article from the *los angeles times.*
16. King John of England signed the magna carta in 1215.
17. My family gave my great aunt bonita a surprise party.
18. R. K. Narayan's story "naga" is very well written.
19. I have enjoyed stories by William Faulkner, especially "spotted horses."
20. I saw a dog growl at his reflection on the television show *america's funniest home videos.*

MODULE 10: CAPITAL LETTERS

MODULE REVIEW

A. Correcting Errors in Capitalization

Each of the following sentences contains errors in capitalization. Write your corrections on the lines provided, and separate your answers with a semicolon.

EX. 1. That woman, dr. olivera, gave a speech on tuesday.
Dr. Olivera; Tuesday

1. sheila said, "my favorite team is the new york mets."

____

2. We ate indian dishes at the restaurant called aroma on route 1.

____

3. The headquarters of the society for ecology restoration is at 1207 seminole highway in madison, Wisconsin.

____

4. Did you know cousin keisha wanted to work for the u.s. secret service someday?

____

5. My family traveled on the subway, called the mbta, when we visited the museum of fine arts in boston.

____

6. The Book *a guide to enjoying wildflowers* was given to me by my uncle jerome.

____

7. I had a coupon for tropicana orange juice, so I went to stop & shop on Route 127.

____

8. what was the best part of your labor day trip to yosemite national park?

____

9. The book *the bluest eye* by african american writer toni morrison is in the Boston public library.

____

10. Alberto ríos wrote a poem called "madre sofía," which I recited at the brown high school talent show.

____

B. Proofreading for Correct Capitalization

For the sentences below, correct the errors in capitalization by drawing a line through each error and writing the correct form above it.

Friday Mr.
EX. [1] On ~~friday mr.~~ Nguyen gave us interesting news.

[1] He said, "this british literature class will plan a medieval banquet." [2] *Medieval* is another name for the middle ages, a period in european history. [3] The banquet will take place in the pérez high school cafeteria, on valentine's day, and we will dress as characters from works we read in class. [4] I have decided to go as sir gawain, from the poem *sir gawain and the green knight*, and my friend nico will go as king Arthur from Sir Thomas Malory's story *Le Morte D'Arthur.* [5] I have invited aunt pearl, who is a photographer for the *neighborhood gazette*, for she thinks our banquet will make a good feature story for the saturday edition.

C. Working Cooperatively to Write a Guidebook

At a recent town meeting, you were elected to prepare a guidebook for newcomers to your neighborhood. Working with a partner, give two specific items that fit into each category below. Explain where they are located, when they are open, and why they are worth knowing about. Write your sentences on your own paper, and be creative and thorough. You don't want people to miss any of the hot spots!

theaters	places to shop
libraries	museums
entertainment areas	historical sites
good places to eat	recreational sites
scenic areas	schools

EX. ***Panda Garden.*** *Enjoy the best Chinese food in the area in an elegantly decorated dining room. Prices are moderate; complete dinner specials include beverages and dessert. Be sure to sample the award-winning spring rolls and lo mein dishes. Panda Garden is located at 223 School Street, just one block from the Loomis Public Library. It is open seven days a week, 11:00 A.M. to 10:00 P.M.*

MODULE 11: PUNCTUATION

END MARKS

An ***end mark*** is a mark of punctuation placed at the end of a sentence. The three kinds of end marks are the period, the question mark, and the exclamation point.

11a A statement (*or* declarative sentence) is followed by a period.

EXAMPLES I have been studying for the algebra quiz all evening.
For our party, Georgia brought latkes, and Lea brought empanadas.

11b A question (*or* interrogative sentence) is followed by a question mark.

EXAMPLES May I borrow that book when you are through?
Shouldn't we leave early, since the weather is bad?

NOTE Be sure to distinguish between a declarative sentence that contains an indirect question and an interrogative sentence, which asks a direct question.

INDIRECT QUESTION She asked me to join the team. [declarative]
DIRECT QUESTION Will you join the team? [interrogative]

11c An exclamation is followed by an exclamation point.

EXAMPLES Wow! What a beautiful sunset!
Oh! We would love to go to the game with you!

Instead of a period or question mark, use an exclamation point after declarative and interrogative sentences that express strong emotion.

EXAMPLES Jake is finally here!
Why won't this rain stop!

11d An imperative sentence is followed by either a period or an exclamation point.

EXAMPLES Please clean this room.
Clean this room now!

An imperative sentence may be stated in the form of a question. However, since its purpose is to give a command or make a request, it should be followed by a period or an exclamation point.

EXAMPLES May I have your undivided attention.
Will you give me your undivided attention!

EXERCISE 1 Correcting Sentences by Adding End Marks

Add the correct end mark to each of the following sentences. [Note: There may be more than one correct way to punctuate a sentence.]

EX. 1. Would you like any help?

1. Students in Giorgio's cooking class made a delicious guacamole dip for their final project
2. Please move the red bicycle into our garage before the rain begins
3. Avery asked if I would please teach him how to do that funny dance
4. What an incredible idea that was
5. Watch where you're going
6. When does Renata begin her paper route
7. That red kimono in the hall closet belonged to my great-grandmother
8. Call the country music station, and request Esperanza's favorite song
9. How surprised you must have been
10. Does your diving watch need a new battery
11. Watch your step
12. She asked you to quiet down
13. Mia will be joining us later in the evening for dinner and for a game of charades
14. Do any of the art projects that are hanging in the school cafeteria belong to you
15. Stop that bus
16. The International Club asked if they could plan a party
17. Could we attend the festival this weekend
18. Ask Mr. Olivera to be a chaperone
19. My cousin just learned how to drive
20. It is disappointing that the town pool will be closed next week
21. How do you expect me to do that
22. Join the choir
23. I asked if I could help with any of the plans
24. Are you bringing Oliver
25. My goodness, you scared me

MODULE 11: PUNCTUATION

ABBREVIATIONS

11e Use periods after most abbreviations.

Abbreviations with Periods	
Personal Names	Susan B. Anthony, W. C. Fields
Titles Used with Names	Dr., Jr., Sr., Mr., Mrs., Ms.
States	N. Mex., Ga., Conn., Wash.
Organizations and Companies	Co., Inc., Corp., Assn.
Addresses	St., Rd., Ave., P.O. Box, Blvd.
Times	A.M., P.M., A.D., B.C.

Some common abbreviations are often written without periods.

EXAMPLES FBI, TV, FDA, oz, ft, lb, cm, kg, ml, VCR, PTA, NAACP

NOTE Two-letter state codes are used only when the ZIP Code is included. Two-letter state codes are **not** followed by periods.

EXAMPLE Austin, TX 78729

When an abbreviation that ends with a period comes at the end of a sentence, do not add another period as an end mark. *Do* add a question mark or an exclamation point if one is needed.

EXAMPLES The artifact was dated 3500 B.C.
Why did he move to St. Louis, Mo.?

NOTE *Inch(es)* is abbreviated ***in.*** to avoid confusing it with ***in,*** the preposition. If you are not sure whether to use periods with an abbreviation, look in a dictionary.

EXERCISE 2 Using Punctuation Correctly in Abbreviations

On your own paper, rewrite the phrases below, using the correct punctuation. If the abbreviation is correct, write *C.*

EX. 1. Dr E Hilario
1. *Dr. E. Hilario*

1. 1 oz of cheddar cheese
2. 54 Hanover St
3. The news program on MTV
4. Ms Feona S Doyle
5. the nature program on PBS at 5:00 P M
6. Rockport Art Assn
7. Anchorage, AK 99502
8. 8 mi to the FBI building
9. Rufus Thompson, Jr
10. PO Box 245

MODULE 11: PUNCTUATION

REVIEW EXERCISE

A. Correcting Punctuation in Sentences

In the sentences below, insert any missing punctuation, and draw a line through any punctuation that is not needed. [Note: There may be more than one correct way to punctuate a sentence.]

EX. 1. I'm so excited to see Ms. Rego again!

1. May I have your attention, please
2. We met about 6:00 P M at Monticello St and Rivera Ave
3. Dr Montel said that our new baby sister weighs 7 lbs and 5 oz
4. That's an amazing C.D.
5. Did you know that Cousin Fernando was joining the Peace Corps
6. Quiet down immediately
7. My family moved to St. Paul, Minn, from Hartford, Conn
8. The measuring tape uses ft on one side and m and c.m. on the other
9. My business is called Child Inc, and it is a popular baby-sitting service
10. I mailed a package to my best friend, Angela, whose address is 1819 Red Oak Circle, Austin, TX 78746
11. Is Mount Caubvick in Labrador more than 15,000 ft high
12. I remember seeing a T.V. show about the F.B.I.
13. Did W E B Du Bois found the NAACP
14. The grocery store moved from Washington St to Jefferson Ave
15. Frank didn't know whether 1 kg. equaled 2.2 lb

B. Working Cooperatively to Write an Advertising Description

Work with a partner to create an idea for an educational board game. Base it on a specific subject, choose a name, and decide on the object of your game. Then with your partner, write an advertising description for your board game. The description, written on your own paper, should include ten sentences that use three of the five punctuation rules introduced at the beginning of this module.

EX. *Name:* *PROFESSOR SCIENCE*
Object: *to answer correctly ten questions from three science areas—animals, plants, earth*
Sentence: Wow! This is a game every kid will love!

COMMAS IN A SERIES

11f Use commas to separate items in a series.

EXAMPLES My sisters and I collect baseball cards, coins, hats, rocks, and stamps. [words]

We found information in reference books, in magazine articles, and in newspaper articles. [phrases]

The school dance will be a success if Sergio sets up a refreshment table, if Maya hires a good band, and if plenty of students attend. [clauses]

NOTE Some words—such as *macaroni and cheese, law and order*, and *peace and quiet*—are paired so often that they may be considered one item in a series.

EXAMPLE My father prepared a delicious meal of steamed broccoli, macaroni and cheese, and apple crisp.

If all items in a series are joined by *and, or*, or *nor*, do not use commas to separate them.

EXAMPLES Neither my brother **nor** my friend **nor** I could coax the puppy from under the bed after the thunderstorm.

On vacation I jogged **and** read books **and** wrote in the journal I had started.

11g Use a comma to separate two or more adjectives preceding a noun, but not after the last adjective before the noun.

EXAMPLE Running that road race was a fun, challenging, exhausting experience.

EXERCISE 3 Correcting Sentences by Adding Commas

Add commas where they belong in the following sentences. If a sentence is correct, write *C* on the line before the sentence.

EX. _____ 1. Doreen has played shortstop, third base, and left field for her baseball team.

_______ 1. You can help that organization by donating money by volunteering your time or by attending fund-raising events.

_______ 2. Marty adopted a large beautiful affectionate cat from the animal shelter.

_______ 3. We packed food canteens blankets flashlights and a tent for our one-night camping trip.

_______ 4. We are looking forward to some fun some adventure and some peace and quiet.

_______ 5. Tell Mercedes she can visit on Tuesday or on Friday or on Sunday afternoon.

_______ 6. I hid the children's prizes in the bushes under some lawn chairs and behind big rocks.

_______ 7. That bakery sells French bread sourdough rolls Portuguese rolls and challah.

_______ 8. Wasn't my apartment humid hot and terribly uncomfortable yesterday afternoon?

_______ 9. I would like some advice about putting up wallpaper painting shutters and repairing cabinet doors.

_______ 10. People swim hike and jog at the park on West Street.

_______ 11. Do you expect many friends family members and neighbors to attend the church bazaar?

_______ 12. Feta cheese tastes wonderful on sandwiches in salads or crumbled on crackers.

_______ 13. The town hired three more police officers so that people could enjoy more protection more peace of mind and more quiet.

_______ 14. It was decided that Martina Sarah and Erin would be in charge of organizing the track-and-field events.

_______ 15. "My favorite magazines are *National Geographic Seventeen* and *Ebony,*" Danielle said.

_______ 16. The spaghetti dinner was sponsored by the Fire Department the Ambulance Association and a local bank.

_______ 17. The map is in the glove compartment under the seat or on the floor.

_______ 18. My report is going to be about one of these topics: South America's writers or modern plays.

_______ 19. We mow lawns clip hedges and water plants for a fair price.

_______ 20. I have a headache because I just took a long crowded noisy bus ride.

MODULE 11: PUNCTUATION

PUNCTUATING INDEPENDENT CLAUSES

11h Use a comma before *and, but, or, nor, for, so,* and *yet* when they join independent clauses.

EXAMPLES Claudia wanted to catch the bus**, but** it had already left.
I want to visit the museum**, and** Jaki wants to go with me.

NOTE The comma may be left out before *and, but, or,* and *nor* if the independent clauses are very short or if the sentence cannot be misunderstood.
EXAMPLE I studied and I did well.

Don't confuse a compound sentence with a simple sentence that has a compound verb.

SIMPLE SENTENCE Ricardo **performs** with the marching band but **conducts** the orchestra. [one independent clause with a compound verb]

COMPOUND SENTENCE Ricardo performs with the marching band, but he conducts the orchestra. [two independent clauses]

11i Independent clauses in a series are usually separated by semicolons. However, commas may separate short independent clauses.

EXAMPLES Before the afternoon tea we put flowers in the vases**;** we vacuumed the rugs**;** and we put linen napkins on each table.
All day long we dusted**,** we polished**,** and we vacuumed.

EXERCISE 4 Correcting Compound Sentences by Adding Commas and Semicolons

In the following sentences, add commas and semicolons where they belong. If a sentence is correct, write *C* on the line before it. [Note: There may be more than one correct way to punctuate a sentence.]

EX. ______ 1. Lorraine loves animals, yet she doesn't own one.

_______ 1. Randy opened the box he removed its contents and he put the box in the recycling bin.

_______ 2. Will you answer the door and listen for the phone?

_______ 3. I love cool weather but Lexi prefers warmer weather.

_______ 4. Roxanne goes for a jog each morning for she wants to stay healthy and strong.

_______ 5. Akim worked hard and he saved his money.

_______ 6. I showed the kitten her new toy yet she didn't seem as interested as I had hoped.

_______ 7. Harriet Tubman ran into many obstacles but she succeeded in making the Underground Railroad a success.

_______ 8. I enjoy writing poetry and listening to different types of music.

_______ 9. We cleaned the room we set up tables and we hung a big sign.

_______ 10. Danya knows the way to the new variety store and she offered to draw a map for us.

_______ 11. I ordered spring rolls and mixed vegetables and I shared them with everyone.

_______ 12. My neighbor Monique has traveled a great deal yet she hasn't taken many photographs.

_______ 13. My friend Estrella moved here from Mexico last year and she often misses her friends back home.

_______ 14. Manatees are large, gentle sea mammals and they are frequently injured by passing motorboats.

_______ 15. Mr. Avery creates beautiful rugs but he rarely sells any of them.

_______ 16. Angie planted the flower seeds and she watered them.

_______ 17. As a child Wilma Rudolph didn't have the use of one of her legs but she later became the gold medalist in track at the 1960 Olympics.

_______ 18. Go to the other vegetable stand because they have the freshest produce they have the best variety and they have the best prices.

_______ 19. "I wanted to attend the reading but I couldn't find the address," Charese said.

_______ 20. Paco dances and he sings.

_______ 21. My cousins from Germany are visiting us for two weeks so we are planning several day trips to show them our historical sites.

_______ 22. Nine pole-vaulters tried to clear the bar but only one succeeded.

_______ 23. The hikers chose an inviting spot near a stream and set up their campsite for no one realized that a skunk family lived nearby.

_______ 24. Jared opened a small restaurant and invited his friends to enjoy a meal at half price.

_______ 25. The visitors were impressed by the empty land the local people took it for granted but all were awed by the Grand Canyon.

MODULE 11: PUNCTUATION

COMMAS WITH NONESSENTIAL ELEMENTS

11j Use commas to set off nonessential clauses and nonessential participial phrases.

A ***nonessential*** (or ***nonrestrictive***) clause or participial phrase is one containing information that isn't needed to understand the main idea of the sentence.

NONESSENTIAL PHRASE My cousin**, walking home one day,** found a large snapping turtle.

NONESSENTIAL CLAUSE That scarf**, which is real silk,** was made in India.

An ***essential*** (or ***restrictive***) phrase or clause is one that cannot be left out without changing the meaning of the sentence. Essential clauses and phrases are not set off by commas. Notice how leaving out the essential clause or phrase would change the meaning of the following sentences.

ESSENTIAL PHRASE A book **written by Maxine Hong Kingston** is about growing up as a Chinese American woman.

ESSENTIAL CLAUSE Vehicles **that do not pass inspection** must be taken off the roads.

NOTE Adjective clauses beginning with *that*, like the one in the example above, are nearly always essential.

EXERCISE 5 Correcting Sentences by Adding Commas

Insert commas where necessary in the following sentences. Then identify each italicized phrase or clause by writing *e.* for *essential* or *n.e.* for *nonessential* on the line before each sentence.

EX. ___*e.*___ 1. The police officer *who was directing traffic* is my aunt.

_______ 1. Frederick Douglass *who taught himself to read and write* was one of the most effective speakers of his time.

_______ 2. The shirt *hanging on the doorknob* belongs to Maris.

_______ 3. Crowds *that are not kept under control* can be dangerous.

_______ 4. Genevieve *who plays the flute and oboe* is in a concert tonight at the town hall.

_______ 5. Have you learned the vocabulary words for the test *which is today*?

_______ 6. Jimmy Carter *who was the thirty-ninth president of the United States* was from Georgia.

_______ 7. I've read wonderful poetry *written by Elizabeth Bishop.*

_______ 8. This tasty recipe *which is made with spinach noodles* is Marta's favorite meal.

_______ 9. How long do you expect this storm *which sounds like a hurricane* to be passing over our town?

_______ 10. The blue-and-white plates *sitting on the table* were given as a gift.

_______ 11. My mother *leaning against the counter* announced that she didn't feel well.

_______ 12. The boy *who is working part time at the market* will be joining us later.

_______ 13. Meals from southern India *which are often vegetarian* are sometimes made with grated coconut.

_______ 14. The basket *woven by my grandfather* sits on the table by the front door.

_______ 15. Any letters *that you place in the mailbox* will definitely go out this afternoon.

_______ 16. The antiques *that are the most valuable* are in the back of the store.

_______ 17. Jasper *swimming in the pond one afternoon* found some beautiful lily pads.

_______ 18. That medication *which is for my allergies* is in the refrigerator drawer.

_______ 19. Erin often makes plans *that change at the last minute.*

_______ 20. Have any of you seen the new monument *which is in the center of the town square*?

_______ 21. The football game *that was on TV on Thanksgiving Day* was as muddy as any I'd ever seen.

_______ 22. The waves *that crashed against the rocky shore* were lovely to hear and to see.

_______ 23. Penelope learned embroidery *which is a difficult skill to learn.*

_______ 24. Washington, D.C. *which is the U.S. capital* is a busy city.

_______ 25. Martín *who walks to school with me* is moving to Kentucky.

MODULE 11: PUNCTUATION

COMMAS WITH INTRODUCTORY ELEMENTS

11k Use a comma after certain introductory elements.

(1) At the beginning of a sentence, use a comma after *yes, no*, and mild exclamations such as *well* and *why.* Interjections such as *wow, yikes*, and *hey*, if not followed by an exclamation point, are also set off by commas.

EXAMPLES No, the restaurant is not closing early this evening.
Well, I was hoping to be home by then.
Hey, didn't we meet at the carnival last year?

(2) Use a comma after an introductory participial phrase.

EXAMPLES **Practicing her guitar one day,** Pasha taught herself to play that song.
Frightened by the loud noise, the baby cried for an hour before falling back to sleep.

(3) Use a comma after two or more introductory prepositional phrases.

EXAMPLE **On the sidewalk behind the school,** squirrels gathered to look for food.

(4) Use a comma after an introductory adverb clause.

EXAMPLE **After you come home from band practice,** please prepare dinner for the family.

EXERCISE 6 Using Commas in Sentences with Introductory Elements

On the line before each of the following sentences, write the word that comes before the missing comma, and place the comma after it. Write *C* if the sentence is correct.

EX. *Yes,* 1. Yes I do know that poem by heart.

________ 1. Practicing every day I learned to speak Spanish well.

________ 2. In the garbage cans behind our house we had ants.

________ 3. Wow I didn't think so many people would arrive for the presentation.

________ 4. In the back of the store's parking lot we saw an interesting purple convertible.

________ 5. Well you look relaxed today.

__________ 6. After the meeting adjourned everyone helped prepare a snack at my apartment.

__________ 7. At midnight we heard a loud thunderstorm.

__________ 8. Singing an original song Raul impressed the spectators.

__________ 9. Staring at a beetle the cat crouched and prepared to pounce.

__________ 10. Next to my locker somebody spilled a container of juice.

__________ 11. When the prairies burned the fire seemed like red buffalo.

__________ 12. In Afghanistan Muslim brides often wear green, the symbol of hope.

__________ 13. Yes that scientist did win an important award.

__________ 14. As you answer each question keep track of your time.

__________ 15. Why that must be the famous movie actor.

__________ 16. In the back of the room the children hung their finger paintings.

__________ 17. Over the front door we hung a watercolor.

__________ 18. Yikes I didn't think anyone was in here!

__________ 19. In the park near the school the boys helped build a short footpath.

__________ 20. Long before the British settled Labrador the Innu people hunted caribou there.

__________ 21. Sailing through the jumps the horse and rider were quite impressive.

__________ 22. After the town meeting people were satisfied.

__________ 23. After we shared many interesting ideas we came up with a plan.

__________ 24. Calling an old friend I dialed the wrong number.

__________ 25. Sarah said, "No I don't need any more help."

__________ 26. Fishing for compliments Elena commented that her hair looked awful.

__________ 27. Running and lifting weights every day Lewis built up his endurance and strength.

__________ 28. Sure I'd be happy to take Sally to the carnival.

__________ 29. Digging through the ice the scientists uncovered the remains of a woolly mammoth.

__________ 30. In the ditch beside the road Danny found a gold coin.

MODULE 11: PUNCTUATION

COMMAS WITH OTHER SENTENCE INTERRUPTERS

11l Use commas to set off elements that interrupt a sentence.

(1) Appositives and appositive phrases are usually set off by commas.

An ***appositive*** is a noun or pronoun that follows another noun or pronoun to identify or explain it. When you set off an appositive element, be sure to include all the words that are part of it.

EXAMPLES Cheryl**, the class president,** is giving a speech today.
I spoke with him**, the teacher,** in the back row.

Sometimes an appositive is used to specify a particular person, place, thing, or idea. Such an appositive is called a ***restrictive appositive.*** Commas are not used to set off restrictive appositives.

EXAMPLES My cousin **Liam** is going to a new high school. [The writer has more than one cousin. The appositive *Liam* specifies which cousin.]
Have you read the novel ***The Fault in Our Stars***? [The appositive *The Fault in Our Stars* specifies the particular novel.]

(2) Use commas to set off words used in direct address.

EXAMPLES **Ida,** do you have my sneakers?
Thank you, **Kalil,** for your dedication and hard work.

(3) Use commas to set off parenthetical expressions.

A ***parenthetical expression*** is a side remark that adds information or relates ideas. Some parenthetical expressions include *nevertheless, for instance, however, that is*, and *therefore.*

EXAMPLES Jackson**, on the other hand,** would make a great assistant. **For instance,** he is kind and charitable.

NOTE A contrasting expression introduced by *not* or *yet* is parenthetical and should be set off by commas.
EXAMPLE His solo provided a simple**, yet elegant,** end to the recital.

EXERCISE 7 Correcting Sentences by Adding Commas

Add commas where they belong in the following sentences. If a sentence is correct, write *C* on the line before the sentence.

EX. _______ 1. Melita of course will help you answer any questions.

_______ 1. The 984-foot Eiffel Tower in Paris was built for the International Exposition of 1889.

_______ 2. Will you be visiting us again soon Ramón?

_______ 3. I talked with Fatima my new science partner.

_______ 4. I know in fact that parking places will be difficult to find on the day after Thanksgiving.

_______ 5. Have you seen the movie *Coco* yet?

_______ 6. Tiffany how long will the sale at Parelli's be going on?

_______ 7. We may on the other hand get better seats at the next show if we wait.

_______ 8. It was Petra not Gary who came up with that clever and very workable plan.

_______ 9. Stella the manager is going to have a word with those uncooperative employees.

_______ 10. Meanwhile everyone will be wondering what is going on.

_______ 11. How many blocks of cheese Meredith will we need for the picnic?

_______ 12. I enjoyed reading the novel *The Chocolate War.*

_______ 13. Generally speaking voter turnout in our town was excellent this year.

_______ 14. I now understand the equation the one on the blackboard better.

_______ 15. "How far north does this train travel Sir?" Mario asked the conductor.

_______ 16. At any rate we have to decide on a new school song for future years.

_______ 17. Mr. Carter that candle maker on Jackson Street is truly a fascinating man.

_______ 18. On the contrary I believe you would be perfect for that role Julian.

_______ 19. Have you seen our affectionate yet independent Scottish terrier?

_______ 20. Cameron please deliver these books to the library at the end of the street.

MODULE 11: PUNCTUATION

OTHER USES OF COMMAS

11m Use commas to separate items in dates and addresses.

EXAMPLES President Abraham Lincoln's Emancipation Proclamation took effect on January 1, 1863.

Thomas Edison opened the world's first motion picture studio on February 1, 1893, in West Orange, New Jersey.

On Friday, October 22, 1 will take a road trip.

Jacob lives at 4405 Tree Lane Road, Savannah, GA 31405.

Send it to Mr. Lu, 125 Boynton Street, New York, NY 10019.

No comma separates the month from the day, the house number from the street name, or the ZIP Code from the two-letter state code. If the day is given before the month or if only the month and the year are given, no comma is used.

EXAMPLES The date on the wedding invitation is 21 September 2019.

The last time my grandmother visited us was April 2019.

11n Use a comma after the salutation of a friendly letter and after the closing of any letter.

EXAMPLES Dear Aunt Lucy, Sincerely,

11o Use a comma after a name followed by an abbreviation such as *Jr., Sr.,* or *M.D.* and after the abbreviation when it is used in a sentence.

EXAMPLE Angelina Valdez, M.D.

Martin Luther King, Jr., was a civil rights leader.

EXERCISE 8 Proofreading Dates, Addresses, and Parts of a Letter for Correct Use of Commas

Add commas where they belong in the following items.

EX. 1. 1500 Madison Avenue, New York, NY 10016

1. P.O. Box 6813 Cambridge MA 02238
2. August 29 1980 in New Haven Connecticut
3. Sincerely yours
4. From September 1 2019 through July 31 2020
5. Circum-Pacific Map Project in Menlo Park CA 94025

6. Dearest Tracey
7. Until January 9 2009
8. Downtown Philadelphia Pennsylvania
9. Teresa Franklin M.D.
10. Dear Marike
11. Talk to Ed Baker Sr. about the window.
12. 975 Mountain View Avenue San Anselmo California
13. All the best
14. Rural Route 12 Lindale Texas
15. P.O. Box 99500 St. Petersburg FL 33743
16. April 9 2008 at 4:00 P.M.
17. Efrem Zimbalist Jr.
18. My Dear Aunt Pepina
19. Dinosaur National Monument in Jensen UT 84035
20. Saturday July 18 through Wednesday August 6
21. Best wishes
22. 15 Cypress Hill Montgomery Street Fort Worth TX 76107
23. University of Wisconsin at 1215 West Dayton Street Madison WI53706
24. on January 1 2010
25. Macon County North Carolina

EXERCISE 9 Proofreading a Letter for Correct Use of Commas

Insert commas where needed in the letter below.

1 June 20 2008

2 Dear Nora
3 This July I will be staying at 2425 Irma Drive Evanston
4 IL 60202. This is the home of our family friend Juana.
5 Remember when I told you about Dr. Juana Delano the
6 veterinarian and her amazing cats? In August I will be visiting
7 my cousins at 995 Oak Circle Wilmette IL 60091, and I'll be
8 home after that.
9 Fondly,
10 Tabia

MODULE 11: PUNCTUATION

MODULE REVIEW

A. Proofreading Sentences for Correct Punctuation

Insert commas and periods and other end marks where needed in the sentences below. If a sentence is correct, write *C* on the line before it.

EX. _____ 1. I bought a large, floppy canvas hat.

_______ 1. Tyrone have you been to Michigan which is a state near the Great Lakes

_______ 2. Yes I went to the Bailey-Matthews Shell Museum at 2499 Windy Palms Road Sanibel Island Florida.

_______ 3. Traveling on a whale-watching ship we saw whales dolphins and many other types of marine life

_______ 4. Dr Jane Goodall a scientist from England went to Africa to study chimpanzees.

_______ 5. Well I invited Catalina Mendez MD to the conference but she already had plans

_______ 6. Wow This old bumpy dusty road needs to be repaved very soon.

_______ 7. After lunch we took the elevator to the top floor and viewed the city.

_______ 8. I want you Lee and Trenell to clean up your desks now

_______ 9. The tourists photographed historical sites ate in local restaurants and bought souvenir postcards.

_______ 10. On Friday January 15 a representative from Profits, Inc will speak to the PTA about fund-raising.

B. Proofreading a Paragraph for Correct Punctuation

In the following paragraph, insert commas where they are needed.

EX. [1] Sitting in a park on a windy day, we saw many kites.

[1] Chung Yang Chieh the Kiteflying Holiday is a special day in China. [2] At dawn boys and their fathers uncles grandfathers and other male relatives climb hills and mountains near their towns. [3] Standing on the mountains they spend the day flying beautiful kites. [4] The kites are brightly colored and people often spend weeks

creating them. [5] Most kites are made of paper some are made of silk and many have intricate designs. [6] One popular design for example is a bat which symbolizes happiness and long life. [7] Instead of counting by months and days the Chinese calendar counts time by the moon so holidays occur on the sixth day of the Sixth Moon or the fourth day of the Fourth Moon. [8] The Kiteflying Holiday occurs on the ninth day of the Ninth Moon which is also called the Chrysanthemum Moon. [9] Yes this holiday is over two thousand years old and it celebrates the legend of a brave family whose village was destroyed. [10] Escaping to the top of the mountain the family survived and lived a prosperous life.

C. Cooperating to Write a Business Plan

You are planning to open a new business. Work with a partner to invent a business name and logo. Then, together, write a brief report to the City Business Council about your plans. Your report might include job descriptions for employees, an analysis of prospective customers, a slogan, and a list of possible products or services. Write ten complete sentences demonstrating at least five of the rules from this module.

EX. *Name of business: Homesweet Homes*

1. *Employees, we believe, are the heart of the company and should be treated well.*

MODULE 12: PUNCTUATION

SEMICOLONS

12a Use a semicolon between independent clauses in a sentence if they are not joined by *and, but, or, nor, for, so,* or *yet.*

EXAMPLE Everyone else in my family loves swimming; I prefer hiking.

When the thoughts in two short sentences are closely related, a semicolon can take the place of the period between them.

EXAMPLES The river is rising rapidly. It's expected to crest by noon. [two simple sentences]
The river is rising rapidly; it's expected to crest by noon.

12b Use a semicolon between independent clauses joined by conjunctive adverbs or transitional expressions.

EXAMPLE Ariel is planning to go to medical school**; however,** she is also interested in ballet.

Commonly Used Conjunctive Adverbs			
accordingly	furthermore	instead	nevertheless
besides	however	meanwhile	otherwise
consequently	indeed	morever	therefore

Commonly Used Transitional Expressions			
as a result	for instance	in fact	in conclusion
for example	in addition	that is	in other words

12c A semicolon (rather than a comma) may be needed to separate independent clauses joined by a coordinating conjunction if commas appear within the clauses.

CONFUSING Karen, Scott, and Jerome went to the concert, but Felicity, Marcus, and Joan went to the play.

CLEAR Karen, Scott, and Jerome went to the concert; but Felicity, Marcus, and Joan went to the play.

12d Use a semicolon between items in a series if the items contain commas.

EXAMPLE The International Club will meet on Tuesday, September 16; Tuesday, September 23; Tuesday, September 30; and Tuesday, October 7.

EXERCISE 1 Correcting Sentences by Adding Semicolons

In each sentence below, replace each incorrect comma with a semicolon.

EX. 1. Usually we go to the mountains in the summer however, this year we went to the ocean.

1. Sharks have a fearsome reputation, however, many kinds of sharks are harmless to people.
2. Mickey Mouse participated in World War II his name was the Allies' password on D-day in 1944.
3. Nakai does his homework as soon as he gets home, otherwise, he would have to fit it in between his chores and his job at the market.
4. The first ascent by humans in a balloon was in 1783 it lasted about twenty-five minutes.
5. Alana has visited Mexico, Guatemala, and Costa Rica, and next year her family is going to Belize and Honduras.
6. I have received letters from my pen pals in London, England; Moscow, Russia; Nairobi, Kenya, and Suva, Fiji.
7. Boudicca was a queen in ancient Britain, she led a revolt against the Romans.
8. Jonas likes the rain, consequently, you can always find him outside during a storm.
9. The native people who live in the Arctic have been called Eskimos by other Native Americans, however, the different Arctic people call themselves by specific tribal names, such as Inuit and Inupiat.
10. When Lady Murasaki Shikibu wrote *The Tale of Genji* around 1000 A.D., Chinese was the official language of Japan, only working people and women were allowed to speak Japanese.
11. Some important wildlife preservation parks are Salonga Reserve, Zaire; Fjordland National Park, New Zealand, Snowdonia National Park, Wales; and the Royal Chiawan Sanctuary, Nepal.
12. First we had dinner, then we went to a movie.
13. The blue whale is the largest mammal, the pigmy shrew and the bumblebee bat are the smallest mammals.
14. More than forty thousand times each year, some part of the earth shakes, moreover, a major earthquake occurs about once a month.
15. Copper, zinc, silver, and mercury are found in Mexico, in addition, in 1974, reserves of oil were discovered.

MODULE 12: PUNCTUATION

COLONS

12e Use a colon to mean "note what follows."

(1) Use a colon before a list of items, especially after expressions like *the following* and *as follows.*

EXAMPLE You will need the following items: a jacket, sturdy boots, a bag lunch, and insect repellent.

NOTE Do not use a colon before a list immediately following a verb or a preposition.

INCORRECT Additional supplies are: a pocketknife, a first-aid kit, a change of clothes, and a snack.

CORRECT Additional supplies are a pocketknife, a first-aid kit, a change of clothes, and a snack.

(2) Use a colon before a long, formal statement or a long quotation.

EXAMPLE In Lorna's opinion, the twenty-first century will bring many new developments: there will be new cures in medicine, new methods of communication, and improved methods of transportation.

12f Use a colon in certain conventional situations.

(1) Use a colon between the hour and minute.

EXAMPLES 9:30 A.M. 8:00 P.M.

(2) Use a colon between module and verse in referring to passages from the Bible.

EXAMPLES Esther 3:5 John 3:16–21

(3) Use a colon after the salutation of a business letter.

EXAMPLES Dear Ms. De Rosa: Dear Madam or Sir:

EXERCISE 2 Correcting Sentences by Adding Colons

In each of the following sentences, add the missing colon. Some sentences may be correct.

EX. 1. These are my favorite writers Jane Austen, Jack London, and Mark Twain.

1. The sermon last Sunday was based on Exodus 7 16.

2. At the market you need to buy these foods eggs, tortillas, tomatoes, and mangoes.
3. The meeting lasted from 1 30 P.M. until 3 45 P.M.
4. When we went whale watching, we saw two types of whales humpback and minke.
5. In her talk, Dr. Jackson quoted these poets Shakespeare, Shelley, Dickinson, and Frost.
6. It is Leviticus 19 18 that talks about loving our neighbors.
7. The bus will leave at 9 30 A.M.
8. I enjoy the following sports skiing, hiking, and rock climbing.
9. When it is 7 00 A.M. in New York City, it is 3 00 P.M. in Moscow.
10. These religions are practiced in China Buddhism, Confucianism, Taoism, and Islam.
11. Some specialties in medicine are psychiatry, dermatology, and pediatrics.
12. For the camping trip you will need to provide these items a sleeping bag, a backpack, and eating utensils.
13. Juanita pointed out these constellations Pegasus, Draco, and Ursa Minor.
14. Food crops in Mexico include beans, corn, and avocados.
15. Write "Dear Mayor Tobey" for the salutation of your business letter.
16. The bus will leave promptly at 6 00 A.M.
17. These are famous American painters Jackson Pollock, Georgia O'Keeffe, and Mary Cassatt.
18. The ancient Inca Empire consisted of much of these present-day countries Ecuador, Peru, Bolivia, and Chile.
19. On our trip we drove through the following states Arizona, Texas, and New Mexico.
20. The senator believes that his district needs funding "What we propose are improvements for the only clinic in the area, a new heating system for the high school, and a central sewage system for the entire district."

MODULE 12: PUNCTUATION

UNDERLINING (ITALICS)

12g Use underlining (italics) for titles of books, plays, periodicals, films, television series, works of art, long musical compositions, ships, aircraft, and spacecraft.

Type of Name	Examples
Books	*Invisible Man, The Rest of Life*
Plays	*The Tempest, Hamilton*
Periodicals	*The Washington Post, The Boston Globe*
Films	*Green Book, Pitch Perfect*
Television series	*The Voice, The Big Bang Theory*
Work of art	*The Thinker, The Ballet Class*
long musical Composition	*The Magic Flute, Tommy*
Ships	*Mayflower*, USS *Iowa*
Aircraft	*Spirit of St Louis, Dreamliner*
Spacecraft	*Discovery, Phoenix*

NOTE Underline (italicize) the title of a poem long enough to be published in a separate volume.

EXAMPLE My older brother is reading John Milton's *Paradise Lost.*

12h Use underlining (italics) for words, letters, and figures referred to as such, and for foreign words.

EXAMPLES The word *Halloween* has two *l*'s and two *e*'s.
The *6* on that address looks like an *8*.
Luminarias are part of the Mexican Christmas tradition.

EXERCISE 3 Correcting Sentences by Adding Underlining (Italics)

Underline all the words and word groups that should be italicized in the following sentences.

EX. 1. For my birthday I got a subscription to National Geographic.

1. Did you see 60 Minutes last night?

2. The Titanic sank after it hit an iceberg.

3. The astronauts landed on the moon in the lunar module Eagle.
4. Her older sister likes to read Popular Science.
5. At the festival they served moo shi, a well known Chinese dish.
6. It was a great thrill to see Salvador Dali's painting The Persistence of Memory.
7. We were lucky to get tickets to see the play Hamilton.
8. José wrote a book report about Born Free, the story of Elsa, the lion cub.
9. At the fair this summer, the first prize was a cruise on the Island Queen.
10. My mother subscribes to The New York Times.
11. Some people mistake the 7 on this sign for a 1.
12. "I will prepare my favorite dessert, Surprise à l'Orange," Nicole said.
13. Lonesome Dove is a western that takes place in the 1800s.
14. One of Pablo Picasso's most famous works is the painting Guernica.
15. You can probably look up that word in The Oxford English Dictionary.
16. Shalom means "hello," "good-bye," and "peace" in Hebrew.
17. Although it has been many years since the book was written, people still enjoy reading the novel Great Expectations.
18. The president travels on Air Force One.
19. At the end of the birthday party, they showed the movie Deadpool.
20. I can never remember if commitment has one t or two.
21. We enjoyed watching the cooking lessons that Rachael Ray presented on 30-Minute Meals
22. Edith Wharton's book The Age of Innocence was made into a movie starring Daniel Day-Lewis and Michelle Pfeiffer.
23. When she was nine, Christina's favorite book was Stuart Little.
24. Do you know anyone who has sailed on the Queen Elizabeth 2?
25. During the weekend, Tomás read three modules from I Know Why the Caged Bird Sings.

MODULE 12: PUNCTUATION

QUOTATION MARKS

12i Use quotation marks both before and after a direct quotation. Begin the quotation with a capital letter.

EXAMPLE "**M**aybe this is the place," Kerry said.

Do not use quotation marks for *indirect quotations.*

DIRECT QUOTATION "May I go now?" Tranh asked. [his exact words]
INDIRECT QUOTATION Tranh asked if he could leave.

12j When a quoted sentence is divided into two parts by an interrupting expression, the second part begins with a small letter.

EXAMPLE "I asked the same question twice," she said, "**a**nd I got two different answers."

NOTE An interrupting expression is not part of a quotation and should never be inside quotation marks. If, however, the second part of a divided quotation is a sentence, it begins with a capital letter.

EXAMPLE "Look at that," Amy said. "**A** light is flashing at sea."

12k A direct quotation is set off from the rest of the sentence by a comma, a question mark, or an exclamation point, but not by a period.

EXAMPLE Jerome said, "The books are packed and ready to be moved."

12l When used with quotation marks, the other marks of punctuation are placed according to the following rules.

(1) A period or comma should always be placed inside the closing quotation marks.

EXAMPLES Josie said, "That's a beautiful weaving."
"I made it myself," Emma replied.

(2) Colons and semicolons are always placed outside closing quotation marks.

EXAMPLE These people have been nominated for "Student of the Year": Tyrone, Marilyn, Barry, Annika, and Vernon.

(3) Question marks and exclamation points are placed inside the closing quotation marks if the quotation is a question or an exclamation; otherwise, they are placed outside.

EXAMPLES "It's cold in here!" Joe exclaimed.
Why did you choose to read "Mending Wall"?

12m When you write dialogue (conversation), begin a new paragraph every time the speaker changes.

EXAMPLE "Did you see that light?" Cecilia asked.

"Yes," Frank admitted reluctantly. They stopped on the trail and looked at each other doubtfully.

"What do you think it was?" she whispered.

12n When a quoted passage consists of more than one paragraph, put quotation marks at the beginning of each paragraph and at the end of the entire passage.

EXAMPLE The news story reported, "Late last night police discovered a broken window at the Cupboard Restaurant.

"The case is still being investigated. Further reports will be published as they become available."

EXERCISE 4 Proofreading Sentences for Quotation Marks

Add quotation marks where they are needed in the sentences below. Some sentences may be correct.

EX. 1. Grandfather said, "I will tell you about the festival of Gai Jatra."

1. Stop! he shouted.
2. Maya said that she is going to make a bird feeder.
3. If you wish, Mrs. Osaka said, I can tell you how the Japanese celebrate Tanabata.
4. Those videos have all been sold, the salesperson said. We may get more later.
5. Don't ever say, I quit!
6. Why did you say, The Martians have landed?
7. Naomi said It's time to light the candles; then she set the candlesticks on the table.
8. Do you like reggae? she asked.
   I don't know he answered. I'm not sure that I know what reggae is.
9. Earthquake! someone shouted, as the ground began to tremble.
10. The detective said, We have looked into these cases, and the first one was easy to solve.
    However, the second case was much more complicated, and I can't promise any answers soon.

12o Use quotation marks to enclose titles of articles, short stories, essays, poems, songs, individual episodes of TV series, and modules and other parts of books and periodicals.

EXAMPLES We read O. Henry's short story "The Gift of the Magi."
Do you know the poem "Mother to Son" by Langston Hughes?

NOTE The titles of long poems and long musical compositions are italicized, not enclosed in quotation marks.

12p Use quotation marks to enclose slang words, technical terms, and other unusual uses of words.

EXAMPLE The technician said he had to check the "wow" and "flutter" on the sound system.

12q Use single quotation marks to enclose a quotation within a quotation.

EXAMPLE She said, "In reply, I will quote our mayor: 'Recycling is a community effort.'"

EXERCISE 5 Correcting Sentences by Adding Quotation Marks

Add quotation marks where they are needed in the following sentences.

EX. 1. She quoted from Robert Frost's poem "The Gift Outright."

1. Rob told me, She said No when I asked if we were disturbing her.
2. Abi memorized Gwendolyn Brooks's poem The Bean Eaters.
3. Sometimes I think awesome is the only adjective my brother knows.
4. Carlos read aloud Module 2, When the Lights Went Out.
5. Do you like using the mouse on this computer?
6. Everyone liked Pete's version of You've Got a Friend.
7. Next week we will study Unit 6, The Geography of Latin America.
8. Your job is to yell Boo! when the lights go out, Alyssa said.
9. Have you read Cassandra, a poem by Louise Bogan?
10. The Storyteller is one of my favorite tales by Saki.

MODULE 12: PUNCTUATION

REVIEW EXERCISE

A. Correcting Sentences by Adding Underlining (Italics)

In each of the sentences below, underline all the words and word groups that should be italicized.

EX. 1. My father reads <u>Sports Illustrated</u> every week.

1. We stood in line a long time to see the painting the Mona Lisa.
2. Daria always watches the reruns of the TV show This Old House.
3. Although it is nearly four centuries old, The Tragedy of Romeo and Juliet is still popular.
4. Carey made a mistake spelling Guadalajara.
5. Do you know if this number is an 8 or a 3?
6. I read an interesting article in Newsweek.
7. To prepare for his role, Daryl read The Miracle Worker twice.
8. This article tells about the 1957 launching of the satellite Sputnik.
9. The movie theater will present a special showing of Casablanca.
10. She described famous shipwrecks, including the sinking of the Titanic.

B. Correcting Sentences by Adding Quotation Marks

In each of the sentences below, add quotation marks where they are needed.

EX. 1. She sang "Sunny Skies."

1. Look out! a voice called as rocks began to fall.
2. Bianca asked, Where is the shop that sells pottery?
3. Rob suggested, Let's try holding a carwash. That usually earns money.
4. I asked Mrs. Savio, Belinda said, and she said, If it rains, the tour will be postponed.
5. Why, he asked, did you cut your hair?
6. Julian replied, Chogna Choeba is a Tibetan festival.
7. Why did he say Be here at nine?
8. In class we studied T. S. Eliot's poem The Love Song of J. Alfred Prufrock.
9. He said that the disk drive was in hyperdrive, or something like that.
10. These students will read Denise Levertov's poem The Quarry Pool: Jena, Pete, and Marcus.

MODULE 12: PUNCTUATION

APOSTROPHES

The ***possessive case*** of a noun or a pronoun shows ownership or relationship.

12r To form the possessive case of a singular noun, add an apostrophe and an *s*. To form the possessive case of a plural noun ending in *s*, add only the apostrophe.

SINGULAR	neighbor**'s** house	Allan**'s** job	bird**'s** nest
PLURAL	dogs**'** owners	teams**'** fans	girls**'** hats

(1) The few plural nouns that do not end in *s* form the possessive case by adding an apostrophe and an *s*.

EXAMPLES children**'s** toys mice**'s** food

(2) A proper name ending in *s* may add only an apostrophe if the name has two or more syllables *and* if the addition of *s* after the apostrophe would make the name awkward to pronounce.

EXAMPLES Achilles**'** armor City of Taos**'** mayor

(3) Many proper names and common nouns ending in *s* add the apostrophe and *s* if the added *s* is pronounced as a separate syllable.

EXAMPLES Chris**'s** locker bus**'s** driver

12s Possessive personal pronouns and the relative pronoun *whose* do not require an apostrophe.

EXAMPLES This is **my** plan. **Whose** idea was this?

12t Indefinite pronouns in the possessive case require an apostrophe and an *s*.

EXAMPLES anyone**'s** choice everyone**'s** idea

12u In compound words, names of organizations and business firms, and words showing joint possession, only the last word is possessive in form.

EXAMPLES Paul and Raoul**'s** science project
the board of directors**'** report

12v When two or more persons possess something individually, each of their names is possessive in form.

EXAMPLES Michael**'s** and Lily**'s** books
the dog**'s** and the cat**'s** collars

EXERCISE 6 Correcting Phrases by Adding Apostrophes

For each of the following phrases, add apostrophes where they are needed. Some phrases may be correct.

EX. 1. a week's pay

1. my uncles book
2. Dan and Marlas class
3. everyones rights
4. Shakespeares sonnets
5. Maviss bicycle
6. Mexicos coastline
7. Kittys and Maxs schedules
8. the hours of practicing
9. the presidents speech
10. Ulysses voyage
11. womens group
12. American Legions pamphlet
13. someones backpack
14. Charless project
15. the Sierra Clubs membership
16. whose pencil
17. the Jenkins house
18. oxens work
19. brother-in-laws new car
20. the two mountaineers courage

EXERCISE 7 Proofreading for Correct Use of Apostrophes

In the following sentences, add apostrophes where they are needed. Some sentences are correct and will need no apostrophe.

EX. 1. Once more, that cat has taken the dog's bone.

1. The editor in chiefs decision is final.
2. Who the winner will be is anyones guess.
3. Do you know if Arkansas capital is Eureka Springs?
4. This mornings paper has a full report about the fire.
5. Joan said, "Those books are ours."
6. Janice and Gwens trip included stops in Moscow and Gorky.
7. Does anyone in your family know the Cherokee language?
8. According to the weather reports, the winds speed was greater than eighty miles per hour.
9. I wrote my report about Xerxes reign in Persia.
10. The mens tennis team will practice at three o'clock.

MODULE 12: PUNCTUATION

DASHES AND PARENTHESES

Most parenthetical elements are set off by commas or by parentheses. Sometimes, though, such elements call for a sharper separation from the rest of the sentence. In such cases, a dash is used.

12w Use a dash to indicate an abrupt break in thought or speech or an unfinished statement or question.

EXAMPLES "Who—" Rhoda began as the door slowly opened.
The results—I am happy to say—are favorable.

12x Use a dash to mean *namely, that is, in other words,* and similar expressions that come before an explanation.

EXAMPLES I speak two other languages—French and Spanish. [*namely*]
The weather was cool—in the seventies—for the first time in weeks. [*that is*]

NOTE Either a dash or a colon is acceptable in the first example above.

12y Use parentheses to enclose material of minor importance in a sentence.

EXAMPLES The child's question ("Why is the sky blue?") stumped his parents.
Our neighbors' three-year-old daughter (she loves the water) swims in the pool with her parents.

EXERCISE 8 Correcting Sentences by Using Dashes and Parentheses

On the line after each of the following sentences, show where dashes and parentheses are needed by writing the word before, the enclosed material, and the word after each set of marks.

EX. 1. Jerome agreed to listen to an opera what a shock if his parents would listen to his rap records.
opera—what a shock—if ____________________

1. Shirley is worried that her grade-point average it's 3.6 is not high enough for her to win a scholarship to the Naval Academy.

____

2. To assemble this machine the instructions are included takes only an hour.

____

3. C. S. Lewis Gloria has read all of his books is her favorite author.

____

4. They decided they had time to visit two places Belize and Costa Rica.

____

5. We went to Oakland it's just across the bay from San Francisco to see the exhibition.

____

6. The date I'm sorry I forgot to tell you has been changed to next week.

____

7. "Why why didn't you tell me?" she asked.

____

8. The cost of the dinner including the tip was much more than Derek had expected.

____

9. They celebrate April First April Fool's Day with great enthusiasm.

____

10. When the plane landed in Israel the flight took thirteen hours, everyone was eager to walk around and breathe the fresh air.

____

11. We went to Quebec the majority of French-speaking Canadians live there to practice our French.

____

12. Her suggestion it was to serve chile con carne and enchiladas was a popular one.

____

13. Han's poem he has just started writing poetry was accepted by the school's literary publication.

____

14. Because the weather was so cold it was below freezing at night we were glad we had warm clothing.

____

15. Do you ever wonder I often do why winter seems to last so long?

____

MODULE 12: PUNCTUATION

MODULE REVIEW

A. Correcting Sentences by Adding Underlining (Italics), Quotation Marks, Colons, or Semicolons

For each of the sentences below, add underlining (italics), quotation marks, colons, or semicolons where they are needed.

EX. 1. We decided to watch the movie Happy Feet again.

1. In its opening performance of the season, the ballet presented Sleeping Beauty.
2. Denise advised, Bring a coat; however, I forgot.
3. Lian said, Grandmother told me; it was fortunate that I asked.
4. He didn't know any Spanish phrases except por favor.
5. As the parade came closer, the people applauded and shouted Hoorah!
6. For the test, you need the following items a pencil, an eraser, scratch paper, and a calculator.
7. That beach is popular in the summer in other words, if you go there, plan to arrive early to get a good spot.
8. The assignment for tomorrow is to read Module 12, Earthquakes and Volcanoes.
9. The plane arrived at 4 15 P.M. exactly.
10. Let's go on, Haki said. The summit can't be far from here.

B. Proofreading for Errors in Punctuation

For each of the following sentences, correct errors in punctuation by adding apostrophes (include *s* if necessary), dashes, quotation marks, or parentheses where they are needed. Write the sentences on your own paper. If the sentence is correct, write *C*.

EX. [1] The doors were already closed I was only ten minutes late when I arrived.

1. *The doors were already closed* (*I was only ten minutes late*) *when I arrived.*

[1] Let me tell you about yesterday school was closed for in-service teacher workshops when Iris wanted me to go cycling with her and her friend, Zuri.

[2] She said, We don't have to go far, Chris; however, I should have known better.

[3] I knew that Zuri and Iris idea of a short ride would be different from mine, but I went along anyway. [4] We rode to the lake a quick hours ride. [5] Then their plans changed.

[6] We could go on to Markleville for lunch, Iris suggested. It's only another ten miles.

[7] What do you think, Zuri? she continued. She wouldn't ask me because I had stretched out in the sun to rest.

[8] I think we should go around the lake first, Zuri answered, then we could ride the back roads they're prettier than the main road to Markleville.

[9] I pointed out that Iris and Zuris bicycles were newer than mine, but I knew nothing would change their minds nothing does when they get an idea. [10] By my tally, we rode fifty miles on their short bike trip.

C. Writing Slogans

You are the owner of a bumper-sticker shop, and you are creating new slogans for your stickers. You need slogans for the following topics:

favorite sports teams
water conservation
recycling
school
vacation spots
clean air
favorite pets

For five of the topics above, write a slogan at least two lines long. Use at least one of the following marks of punctuation in each slogan: semicolons, colons, italics, quotation marks, apostrophes, dashes, and parentheses. Use a variety of punctuation marks in your slogans.

EX. 1. *Clean air—*
Dear Sir or Madam (*as the case may be*):
Do you want clean air? Then plant a tree.

MODULE 13: SPELLING

THE DICTIONARY

A dictionary entry is divided into several parts. Study the parts of the sample dictionary entry below

1 2 3 4 5

im • prove (im proov'), ***vt.*** **–proved', –prov'ing** [earlier *improw* < Anglo-Fr

5 6

emprower < *en-*, in + *prou*, gain, advantage] **1.** to raise to a better quality or

6 7

condition; make better [to *improve* a method] **2.** to make (land or structures)

8

more valuable by cultivation, construction, etc. **3.** [Now Rare] to use

8

profitably or to good advantage —***vi.*** to become better in quality or condition

—**improve on** (or **upon**) to do or make better than, as by additions or

9

changes **—im•prov'a•bil'i•ty *n.* —im•prov'a•ble *adj.* —im•prov'•er *n.***

10

***SYN.* better, ameliorate *ANT.* worsen, impair**

1. **Entry word.** The entry word shows how the word is spelled and how it is divided into syllables. The entry word may also show capitalization and alternate spellings.
2. **Pronunciation.** The pronunciation is shown by the use of accent marks, phonetic symbols, or diacritical marks. A pronunciation key explains the meaning of diacritical marks and other phonetic symbols.
3. **Part-of-speech labels.** These labels are usually abbreviated and show how the entry word should be used in a sentence. Some words may be used as more than one part of speech. In this case, a part-of-speech label is placed in front of each numbered or lettered series.
4. **Other forms.** An entry may also show spellings of plural forms of nouns, tenses of verbs, or the comparative forms of adjectives and adverbs.
5. **Etymology.** The ***etymology*** is the origin and history of a word. It tells how the word (or its parts) came into the English language and how the word has changed over time.

6. **Definitions.** If there is more than one meaning, definitions are numbered or lettered.
7. **Sample usage.** Phrases or sentences may demonstrate how the defined word is used.
8. **Special usage labels.** These labels identify words that have special meanings or are used in special ways in certain situations.
9. **Related word forms.** These are various forms of the entry word, usually created by adding suffixes or prefixes.
10. **Synonyms and antonyms.** Words similar in meaning are ***synonyms.*** Words opposite in meaning are ***antonyms.*** Synonyms and antonyms may appear at the ends of some word entries.

EXERCISE 1 Using a Dictionary

Use a dictionary to answer the following questions.

EX. 1. How many syllables are in the word *spectacular*? ___*four*___

1. What is the spelling for the plural form of *tomato*? ______________
2. How is the word *humorous* divided into syllables? ______________

____

3. What is the past tense of *awake?* ______________
4. Give three different meanings for the word *box.* ______________

____

5. What is the etymology of the word *kindergarten?* ______________

____

EXERCISE 2 Writing Words with Alternate Spellings

For each word below, write the alternate spellings on the line before the word.

EX. ___*archaeology*___ 1. archeology

______________ 1. monolog

______________ 2. eerie

______________ 3. Hanukkah

______________ 4. enthrall

______________ 5. theater

MODULE 13: SPELLING

SPELLING RULES

ie* and *ei

13a Write *ie* when the sound is long *e*, except after *c*.

LONG *E*	believe	chief	field	niece
AFTER *C*	conceit	deceive	perceive	receipt
EXCEPTIONS	either	leisure	neither	seize

13b Write *ei* when the sound is not long *e* and especially when the sound is long *a*.

EXAMPLES	forfeit	freight	height	neighbor
EXCEPTIONS	friend	lie	mischief	pie

–cede, –ceed,* and *–sede

13c The only English word that ends in *–sede* is *supersede.* The only words that end in *–ceed* are *exceed, proceed,* and *succeed.* All other words with this sound end in *–cede.*

EXAMPLES con**cede** inter**cede** pre**cede** re**cede**

EXERCISE 3 Writing Words with *ie* and *ei*

On the line in each word, write the letters *ie* or *ei* to spell each word correctly. Use a dictionary as needed.

EX. 1. for *ei* gn

1. p_____ ce
2. w_____ rd
3. cash _____ r
4. _____ ght
5. sh_____ ld
6. gr_____ f
7. br_____ f
8. h_____ r
9. th_____ f
10. dec _____ t
11. y_____ ld
12. rec _____ ve
13. b_____ ge
14. conc _____ t
15. c_____ ling
16. th_____ r
17. v_____ l
18. counterf_____ t
19. p _____ rce
20. sl_____ gh

EXERCISE 4 Proofreading a Paragraph to Correct Spelling Errors

In the paragraph below, draw a line through the ten incorrectly spelled words. Write the correct spelling above each incorrect word.

friend

EX. [1] My ~~freind~~ Ashanti and I want to visit the South Pole.

[1] It may seem wierd that we want to spend time in a place that averages -72° Fahrenheit in the winter. [2] However, we both want to sucede in the field of astronomy someday. [3] The South Pole has been recieving attention from astronomers all over the world. [4] Astronomers beleive that Antarctica, the land area surrounding the South Pole, is one of the best places in the world for astronomical observations. [5] The area's altitude, or hieght above sea level, is one reason it provides such accurate observations. [6] Ashanti read a breif article about how the area's low temperatures also improve observations. [7] Scientists do conceed that some of their instruments may not work as well in this extreme cold. [8] Niether Ashanti nor I can imagine what it would be like to visit a place that is always covered with ice. [9] A freindly professor at a nearby college showed us pictures of the Amundsen-Scott South Pole Base, which will eventually have one of the first research facilities in Antarctica. [10] Once Ashanti and I get to the South Pole, maybe we will procede to work there.

MODULE 13: SPELLING

PREFIXES AND SUFFIXES

13d When a prefix is added to a word, the spelling of the original word remains the same.

EXAMPLES mis + spell = **mis**spell il + legible = **il**legible
un + sure = **un**sure dis + advantage = **dis**advantage

13e When the suffix *–ly* or *–ness* is added to a word, the spelling of the original word usually remains the same.

EXAMPLES fit + ness = fit**ness** kind + ness = kind**ness**
swift + ly = swift**ly** usual + ly = usual**ly**
dry + ly = dry**ly** shy + ness = shy**ness**

EXCEPTION For most words that end in *y* and have more than one syllable, change the *y* to *i* before adding *–ly* or *–ness.*

EXAMPLES steady + ness = stead**iness** busy + ly = bus**ily**

13f Drop the final silent *e* before adding a suffix that begins with a vowel.

EXAMPLES tame + est = tam**est** bake + ing = bak**ing**
remove + able = remov**able** safe + er = saf**er**

EXCEPTION Keep the silent *e* in words ending in *ce* and *ge* before a suffix beginning with *a* or *o.*

EXAMPLES service + able = servic**eable**
advantage + ous = advantag**eous**

EXCEPTION To avoid confusion with other words, keep the final silent *e* in some words.
EXAMPLES dyeing, dying
singeing, singing

13g Keep the final silent *e* before adding a suffix that begins with a consonant.

EXAMPLES use + less = use**less** advertise + ment = advertise**ment**
late + ly = late**ly**

EXCEPTIONS judge + ment = judg**ment** true + ly = tru**ly**

EXERCISE 5 Spelling Words with Prefixes and Suffixes

On the lines below, add the given prefix or suffix to each of the words.

EX. 1. il + legal *illegal*

1. sincere + ly ________
2. un + sure ________
3. sudden + ly ________
4. ir + responsible ________
5. thoughtful + ly ________
6. writ + ing ________
7. mis + understand ________
8. insure + er ________
9. rake + ing ________
10. de + compress ________
11. im + mature ________
12. careful + ly ________
13. un + nerve ________
14. ready + ness ________
15. re + arrange ________
16. over + run ________
17. paste + ing ________
18. happy + ly ________
19. dis + satisfied ________
20. waste + ed ________

EXERCISE 6 Spelling Words with Suffixes

On the lines below, add the given suffix to each of the words.

EX. 1. nice + er *nicer*

1. excite + ment ________
2. dye + ing ________
3. slow + ly ________
4. advance + ing ________
5. type + ist ________
6. cold + ness ________
7. make + ing ________
8. true + ly ________
9. take + en ________
10. courage + ous ________
11. approve + al ________
12. mine + ed ________
13. vote + ing ________
14. safe + est ________
15. usual + ly ________
16. nine + ty ________
17. page + ing ________
18. gentle + ness ________
19. love + able ________
20. hope + ful ________

13h **When a word ends in *y* preceded by a consonant, change the *y* to *i* before any suffix except one beginning with *i.***

EXAMPLES study + ing = study**ing** bury + al = buri**al**
lively + er = livel**ier** tasty + est = tast**iest**

13i **When a word ends in *y* preceded by a vowel, simply add the suffix.**

EXAMPLES pay + ment = pay**ment** stay + ed = stay**ed**
EXCEPTIONS say + ed = sa**id** day + ly = da**ily**

13j **Double the final consonant before a suffix that begins with a vowel if the word (1) has only one syllable or is accented on the last syllable *and* (2) ends in a *single* consonant preceded by a *single* vowel.**

EXAMPLES mad + est = ma**dd**est begin + ing = begi**nn**ing
ship + ed = shi**pp**ed stop + er = sto**pp**er

Otherwise, simply add the suffix.

EXAMPLES differ + ence = difference cold + er = colder
near + est = nearest sail + ing = sailing

EXERCISE 7 Spelling Words with Suffixes

On the lines below, add the given suffix to each of the words.

EX. 1. glad + est *gladdest*

1. trap + ed ____________________
2. misty + er ____________________
3. think + ing ____________________
4. gay + ly ____________________
5. worry + ing ____________________
6. mop + ing ____________________
7. sip + ing ____________________
8. clean + er ____________________
9. fluffy + er ____________________
10. stoop + ed ____________________

EXERCISE 8 Proofreading to Correct Spelling in a Paragraph

In the paragraph below, draw a line through each incorrectly spelled word. Write the correct spelling above the incorrect word. [Note: Not every sentence contains a spelling error.]

beautiful

EX. [1] One afternoon Kavon and I found a ~~beautyful~~ kitten alone in an alley.

[1] The animal was busyly cleaning its paws with its rough tongue. [2] The idea that someone would abandon this helpless creature was inconceivable to us, so we tryed to find the owner. [3] We brought the black-and-white kitten some food and a rubber ball, and it seemed happyer. [4] Kavon made some flyers, and he was hopeful that the owner would see one of them. [5] Days went by, however, and we were begining to think we'd need another plan. [6] The kitten would wait for us anxioussly each day and would hungryly nibble the cat food. [7] We pityed the animal, but neither one of us was able to provide a home, since my brother had allergies and Kavon owned two dogs. [8] Eventually, we received a call from someone who wanted to adopt the kitten. [9] The caller, who owned a small bookstore, sayed the cat might be happy climbing on the shelves, lookking out the front window, and lounging in front of the store's wood-burning stove. [10] Now, when we walk by the store dayly on our way home from school, the kitten stares fiercely out the store window, as if to guard its interesting new home.

MODULE 13: SPELLING

PLURALS OF NOUNS

13k Form the plurals of most English nouns by adding *–s*.

SINGULAR	pen	arcade	book	rabbit	clock	plate
PLURAL	pen**s**	arcade**s**	book**s**	rabbit**s**	clock**s**	plate**s**

13l To form the plurals of other nouns, follow these rules.

(1) If the noun ends in *s, x, z, ch,* or *sh,* add *–es.*

SINGULAR	glass	box	waltz	bench	wish
PLURAL	glass**es**	box**es**	waltz**es**	bench**es**	wish**es**

NOTE Proper nouns usually follow these rules, too.

EXAMPLES the Jorden**ses** the Manx**es**
the Sánchez**es** the Frankovich**es**

(2) If the noun ends in *y* preceded by a consonant, change the *y* to *i* and add *–es.* If the noun ends in *y* preceded by a vowel, add *s.*

SINGULAR	city	jury	penny	spy	essay	Sunday
PLURAL	cit**ies**	jur**ies**	penn**ies**	sp**ies**	essay**s**	Sunday**s**

EXCEPTION The plurals of proper nouns: the Kennedys, the Lipskys

(3) For some nouns ending in *f* or *fe,* change the *f* to *v* and add *–s* or *–es.*

SINGULAR	belief	fife	knife	leaf	wife
PLURAL	belief**s**	fife**s**	kni**ves**	lea**ves**	wi**ves**

NOTE Noticing how the plural is pronounced will help you remember whether to change the *f* to *v*.

(4) If the noun ends in *o* preceded by a consonant, add *–es.* If the noun ends in *o* preceded by a vowel, add *s.*

SINGULAR	tomato	hero	patio	rodeo
PLURAL	tomato**es**	hero**es**	patio**s**	rodeo**s**

Nouns for musical terms that end in *o* preceded by a consonant form their plurals by adding *s*.

SINGULAR	solo	cello	contralto
PLURAL	solo**s**	cello**s**	contralto**s**

Some nouns that end in *o* preceded by a consonant have two plural forms.

EXAMPLES mosquito**es** *or* mosquito**s** cargo**es** *or* cargo**s**

(5) The plurals of some nouns are formed in irregular ways.

SINGULAR	child	foot	ox	tooth	woman
PLURAL	child**ren**	f**ee**t	ox**en**	t**ee**th	wom**e**n

(6) Some nouns have the same form in both the singular and the plural.

EXAMPLES deer falafel Japanese trout

(7) If a compound noun is written as one word, form the plural by adding *–s* or *–es*.

SINGULAR	fistful	oilskin	toolbox
PLURAL	fistful**s**	oilskin**s**	toolbox**es**

(8) If a compound noun is hyphenated, or is written as two or three words, make the modified noun plural.

SINGULAR	editor in chief	runner-up	sea gull
PLURAL	editor**s** in chief	runner**s**-up	sea gull**s**

(9) Some nouns borrowed from other languages form their plurals as they do in the original language.

SINGULAR	alumnus	datum	vertebra
PLURAL	alumn**i**	dat**a**	vertebra**e**

(10) To form the plurals of numerals, most capital letters, symbols, and words used as words, add either *–s* or an apostrophe and *–s*.

EXAMPLES Are all of your *t***s** (*or t***'s**) crossed?
Pinga studied the politics of the late 1960**s** (*or* 1960**'s**).

To prevent confusion, always use both an apostrophe and an s to form the plurals of lowercase letters, certain capital letters, and some words used as words.

EXAMPLES The word *Mississippi* has four *s***'s** and four *i***'s**. [Without an apostrophe, the plural of the the letter *i* would look like the word *is.*]

All the *her***'s** in his letter have clear antecedents. [Without the apostrophe, the plural of the word *her* could be confused with the possessive pronoun *hers.*]

EXERCISE 9 Spelling the Plurals of Nouns

On your own paper, write the correct plural form of each of the following nouns.

EX. 1. ax
1. *axes*

1. trench
2. area
3. Pérez
4. soprano
5. life
6. valley
7. Daly
8. woman
9. sheep
10. spoonful
11. blue jay
12. father-in-law
13. crisis
14. 1800
15. rash
16. echo
17. stereo
18. *e*
19. &
20. checkbook

EXERCISE 10 Identifying Incorrect Spelling

Each sentence below contains at least two spelling errors. Draw a line through each incorrectly spelled word, and write the correct spelling above the misspelled word.

Katzes
EX. 1. When the ~~Katzs~~ went on vacation, they had to find someone to take care of
geese
their ~~gooses~~ and goats.

1. The twinses worked for two days on their taxs.
2. All over town, people tuned their radioes to the local station to hear Ella sing her soloes.
3. Mr. Reilly went with the other Reillies to pick berrys.
4. Under the pile of branchs, Irma found a family of mouses.
5. It seemed as though all the childs in those two classes were missing front tooths.
6. Ruth's sister-in-laws spent the morning raking and burning leafs.
7. The Japaneses staying in town for the summer are very fond of Mrs. Myers' apple pie's.
8. The mens arrived promptly at seven, carrying their toolsbox.
9. Keep adding fistsful of soil until the gladiolus are snug in the ground.
10. At the reunion, the alumnuses will enjoy remembering the 1970es.
11. Inside the main building on campus, there is one room where the awardes and trophys of the college teams are displayed.
12. All the six-years-old enjoyed playing with the puppys.
13. With lunch, Mavis had two bunchs of grapes and two handsful of raisins.
14. To set a place for everyone at the table, you will need six knifes and six forkes.
15. In her vegetable garden, Tanya grew tomatos, peppers, and radishs.

MODULE 13: SPELLING

SPELLING NUMBERS

13m Always spell out a number that begins a sentence.

EXAMPLE **Four hundred fifty** students filed into the auditorium.

13n Within a sentence, spell out numbers that can be written in one or two words; use numerals for other numbers.

EXAMPLES Wyatt baked **twenty-five** loaves of bread last weekend.

I guessed that the cheese wheel weighed **125** pounds.

EXCEPTION If you have some numbers of one or two words and some of more than two words, use numerals for all of them.

EXAMPLE The count shows **143** votes for and **80** votes against.

13o Spell out numbers used to indicate order.

EXAMPLE The field hockey team is **fourth** in the division.

EXCEPTION Use numerals for dates when you include the name of the month.

EXAMPLE Grandmother was born on July **4, 1929.**

EXERCISE 11 Spelling Numbers

On your own paper, write five original sentences, following the directions provided below.

EX. 1. Include information about your pet winning the top prize in the pet show.

1. *My dog Sherman won first prize in the pet show this fall.*

1. Begin the sentence with a number.
2. Include two numbers that can be written in one or two words.
3. Include three numbers, one of which can be written in one or two words and two of which can be written in more than two words.
4. Use a number to indicate the place, or rank in class, of a person graduating from high school.
5. Give the month and date of your birthday.

MODULE 13: SPELLING

MODULE REVIEW

A. Correcting Spelling Errors in Sentences

Draw a line through the misspelled word in each sentence below, and write the misspelled word correctly on the line before the sentence.

EX. ___*foreign*___ 1. Molly wants to collect ~~foriegn~~ coins.

______________ 1. Many citys will have a parade on Thanksgiving Day.

______________ 2. The Martínezs fed the family cat while we were away last month.

______________ 3. Vanessa will be haveing a recital in December.

______________ 4. The audience proceded to the lobby for refreshments.

______________ 5. We collected a large amount of datums for our history presentation.

______________ 6. I bought two wooden jewelry boxs at the craft fair.

______________ 7. My baby brother will be steadyer on his feet in another few months.

______________ 8. "The weather is usualy warmer this time of year," the announcer stated.

______________ 9. Kylie and Miguel are both editor in chiefs of the school literary magazine.

______________ 10. My freind Gloria moved here last year from El Salvador.

B. Proofreading a Paragraph to Correct Spelling Errors

In the following paragraph, draw a line through each misspelled word. Write the correct spelling above the misspelled word.

EX. [1] One of my sister's birthday ~~wishs~~ *wishes* was to take a trip to New York City.

[1] My sister was the happyest person in the world as we took a liesurely drive to the city. [2] When we arrived, she was still decideing whether to visit the Statue of Liberty first or to go souvenir shoping. [3] Then we came across an advertisment for the Liberty Science Center close by in Jersey City, New Jersey. [4] My sister decided that visitting this center, which opened on January twenty-fourth, 1993, would be a

great way to spend part of her special day. [5] My parents agreed, and we ended up stayying there the entire day. [6] It was an exciting place because most of the displayes provided hands-on experience. [7] The top floor focussed on the environment, and looker-ons could handle small animals and learn how to predict weather. [8] Other floors had unnusual exhibits about health and inventtions. [9] The center also had a theater with a screen that was eight storys tall. [10] My sister's favorite part of the visit was talking with the "bug lady," an insect speciallist who had a fascinating collection of spiders and giant cockroaches.

C. Using Correct Spelling

You are an exchange student in a foreign country, and you have been assigned to run a spelling workshop for students your age who are learning English. Select two spelling rules from this module to teach to the students. On your own paper, write each rule, and provide examples and an exercise to check students' understanding of the rule. Each exercise should contain five questions or items for students to complete. Write answers for each exercise on a separate piece of paper.

EX. *1. RULE: To form the plural of a noun that ends in y preceded by a consonant, change the y to i and add –es.*

EXAMPLES: *city* *spy* *penny*

cities *spies* *pennies*

EXCEPTIONS: The plurals of proper nouns: the Bailys

EXERCISE: Form plurals of the following words.

1. fly *3. cry* *5. Murphy*

2. sty *4. jelly*

ANSWERS:

1. flies *3. cries* *5. Murphys*

2. sties *4. jellies*